New Brunswick Was His Country

The Life of William Francis Ganong

RONALD REES

NIMBUS
PUBLISHING
NIMBUS.CA

Nimbus Publishing Limited
3731 Mackintosh St, Halifax, NS, B3K 5A5
(902) 455-4286 nimbus.ca

Printed and bound in Canada

NB1234

Cover photo: W. F. Ganong beside the Little Southwest Miramichi River in 1901.
(New Brunswick Museum, Ganong Collection: 1987-17-1218-169)

Cover design: Jenn Embree
Interior design: John van der Woude, JVDW Designs

Library and Archives Canada Cataloguing in Publication
    Rees, Ronald, 1935-, author
    New Brunswick was his country : the life of William
    Francis Ganong / Ronald Rees.
    Includes bibliographical references and index.
    Issued in print and electronic formats.
    ISBN 978-1-77108-448-2 (paperback).—ISBN 978-1-77108-449-9 (html)

1. Ganong, William F. (William Francis), 1864-1941. 2. Botanists—New
Brunswick—Biography. 3. Scholars—New Brunswick—Biography. 4. New
Brunswick—History. 5. New Brunswick—Biography. I. Title.

QK31.G33R48 2016   580.92   C2016-903742-8
                               C2016-903743-6

Canada

Canada Council   Conseil des arts
for the Arts   du Canada

Nimbus Publishing acknowledges the financial support for its publishing activities
from the Government of Canada through the Canada Book Fund (CBF) and the
Canada Council for the Arts, and from the Province of Nova Scotia. We are pleased
to work in partnership with the Province of Nova Scotia to develop and promote our
creative industries for the benefit of all Nova Scotians.

MIX
Paper from
responsible sources
FSC   FSC® C103113
www.fsc.org

To David Erskine

TABLE OF CONTENTS

INTRODUCTION

A few months after his return from central Europe, where he had spent a winter studying in Munich and several weeks walking in the most picturesque parts of the Tyrol and the Swiss Alps, William Francis Ganong and his brother Edwin canoed down the Lepreau, a river in New Brunswick that flows into the Bay of Fundy. When idling in a burnt-over stretch of the river, where the blackened mosses and spruce trunks presaged the shelled woods of the First World War, Ganong turned to his brother and said, apparently without a trace of irony, "How homesick I was for scenes such as this." Ganong never returned to Europe, and when asked why, he answered lightly that there were places in New Brunswick that he still had not seen.

My aim here is to chronicle that devotion. For fifty summers Ganong returned to his home province from Northampton, Massachusetts—where he was Professor of Botany at Smith College—to conduct fieldwork in physiography and natural and social history. He wrote about these ceaselessly. After Ganong's death, Alan Rayburn, a geographer with the federal government in Ottawa, compiled an inventory of his published writings. It amounted to more than six hundred separate items ranging from books to book-length monographs, translations, and hundreds of articles in journals, magazines, and newspapers. Ganong wrote more than many, perhaps most, have ever read, even before the digital age. The range of his interests is as arresting as the volume of his writing: botany, zoology, physiography, cartography, and native languages were all within his reach. As Michael Caron, the author of an excellent thesis on Ganong, remarked, he was a one-man army of scholars.

His great interest, subsuming all the others, was New Brunswick. In a sequence broken only by a two-year sojourn in Europe and the year of the birth of his son, Ganong returned each summer to conduct field research. After leaving New Brunswick, he was first a student and then an instructor at Harvard, and went on to become a professor and chair of the botany department of Smith College, where he remained until his retirement. In 1908, he was elected president of the Botanical Society of America and for nine years was the corresponding secretary for the American Society of Plant Morphology and Physiology. For his work in plant physiology, the society awarded him the Charles Reid Barnes Life Membership in 1940.

Anyone with a passing interest in the natural, social, or settlement history of New Brunswick and the Maritimes will have heard of W. F. Ganong. He is routinely described, in an appellation that hasn't changed since his death in 1941, as New Brunswick's greatest scholar. Mention his name and there will be a murmur or nod of recognition, but extend the exchange and more often than not you'll discover that knowledge of him is paint thin.

He would, however, have taken great care to disabuse anyone of the idea that he was a neglected scholar in his own land. For his books and academic writing his alma mater, the University of New Brunswick, awarded him an honorary Ph.D. and LL.D., and many years after his death a new science building on the Saint John campus was named after him. In 1931, the Royal Society of Canada awarded him the J. B. Tyrrell Historical Medal for his historical research. A few academics have acknowledged his achievements in essays and articles and by collecting and publishing his writings on the cartography of the North Atlantic. But many more fail to mention him at all. Only three copies of two theses that his work inspired, written for the universities of Kansas and Maine, ever found their way into libraries in Canada. One is in the Archives and Special Collections room of the Harriet Irving Library in Fredericton, and the other two are in the Archives and Research Library of the New Brunswick Museum in Saint John. One of the latter was a donation by a member of Ganong's family. None can be borrowed and there are no microfilm or microfiche copies anywhere.

Why this grudging recognition? Ganong's misfortune was to straddle two countries and several fields of research, which he was careful to keep separate. In winter he was a distinguished professor of botany at Smith College in Northampton, Massachusetts, and in summer he was a quiet fieldworker in New Brunswick. His life was so thoroughly compartmentalized that fellow workers in one compartment could not see into the next. The historians at Smith knew nothing of his work on the history of cartography or on the settlement history of New Brunswick. Quite some time after Ganong's second marriage, to Anna Hobbet, Colonel Martin, head of the map division of the Library of Congress, remarked to his wife, Laura, that he had sensed the professor of botany at Smith College, whom her good friend Anna had married, was also the eminent cartographer. Had Ganong been interested in fame—which he decidedly was not—his mistake was to describe his New Brunswick and Maritime studies as a pastime, a diversion from mainstream botany. He joined relatively few professional societies, attended few conventions, did not seek research and travel grants, or covet and collect academic honours. He was as unlike the modern networking, career-oriented academic as it is possible to be.

Aside from a profound disinterest in promoting himself, Ganong was a victim of that classic disjunct: wrong place, wrong time. In Canada, unlike Great Britain, there was no leisured class to establish a tradition of private or independent scholarship: no Gibbons, MacCauleys, or Cecil Woodham Smiths in history, and no Davys or Darwins in the natural sciences. Sir William Logan, the founding director of the Canadian Geological Survey, had no degree of any sort, but made his reputation as a geologist in Wales and England before returning to Canada. Ganong's other misfortune was to live in an era that saw the emergence of the first professional historians and the anointment of the Ph.D. as the *sine qua non* of scholarship. Ganong had one, but it was not in history. Unlike professional historians, he had no ostensible interest in the most fashionable subjects of the time: the building of Canada and the forging of a national identity.

Like many of the French and Flemish historians and geographers, he concentrated on the history and geography of a particular place, going deep rather than wide. He made the point more than once, most emphatically in the introduction to his monograph "The Boundaries of New Brunswick" written for the *Transactions of the Royal Society of Canada*: "I should add that this work, like its predecessors in this series, by no means attempts to discuss those larger issues of the subject which interest historians in general, but is intended to treat it fully from the point of view of local history and geography."

Yet another mistake, had he been career-oriented, was to write even many of his scholarly papers for interested non-specialist readers as well as the university-educated. His informants often were people he met in the fields, farms, and woods from whom he felt no distance but to whom he felt a great obligation. He had a strong sense of public service manifested by his support for lay historical and scientific societies, and his pivotal role in the founding of the New Brunswick Museum.

To honour the predilections of its subject, this text is written for Ganong's audience: the ordinary reader interested in the natural and settlement history of New Brunswick and the working life of its most extraordinary scholar. It is an appreciation of Ganong's work rather than the exhaustive critical assessment that much of it warrants, but that is an assignment for a younger, more ambitious pen than mine.

Chapter 1

⚬ஒ௦⊙ ⊙௦ஒ⚬

THE EDUCATION OF
A NATURALIST

*"Whatever concerns my country, interests me;
I follow nature, with truth my guide."*[1]

N ew Brunswick was W. F. Ganong's country. He was born on February 19, 1864, in Carleton, West Saint John, the eldest of seven children—five boys and two girls—of parents James Ganong and Susan Brittain. Both parents were descendants of United Empire Loyalists who arrived in Saint John with the Spring Fleet of 1783, New Brunswick's *Mayflower.* Ganong's first American ancestor was Jean Guenon, a Huguenot who came to America in 1657 and settled in New York. When Ganong was nine, the family moved to St. Stephen, near the mouth of the St. Croix River, where his father and his uncle, Gilbert Ganong, opened a high-end grocery and confectionery store. Across the river were Maine and the town and port of Calais.

---

1 The maxim, which Ganong liked to cite, on the title page of Peter Fisher's *Sketches of New Brunswick* (1825, revised in 1838). Fisher was the province's first historian.

Groceries did poorly in blue-collar St. Stephen, but candy, to everyone's surprise, sold well. Within a few years, Gilbert and James began manufacturing their own with sugar, molasses, and coconut imported from the West Indies. St. Stephen in the 1870s was still a functioning port with West Indian connections from its once-massive lumber trade. The town also had good rail connections with New England and the rest of Canada. Candy manufacturing flourished, and does still. With profits boosted by a post-Confederation (1867) tariff wall designed to protect Maritime industries, the brothers were also able to build a successful soap factory. Surprise Soap sold throughout the country, and by 1882 James Ganong was mayor of St. Stephen.

There would have been expectations, or hope at least, that James and Susan's first-born son would take to business, but it must have been evident early on that he would not. Summers were spent not on the factory floor, but collecting and classifying rocks, shells, and butterflies on St. Croix River and Belleisle Bay, an inlet of the St. John River. Ganong's grandparents homesteaded at Springfield on the Belleisle, near Kingston, and both his grandfather and father were outdoorsmen and naturalists. To scour the riverbed he made a simple dredge, and to measure distances on land (estimates wouldn't do) he made a clacking device that registered the revolution of a carriage wheel. Rocks, shells, and butterflies were carefully listed, labelled, or mounted and filed away.

He was obsessively orderly. Even agreements with his siblings were recorded: "I (Willie Ganong) Promise to give Eddie Ganong on the 23d August 1877 a pocket book for which I gave him a ball to be kept. [Signed] Willie and Eddie Ganong." Household chores, five per month assigned to each sibling, were also listed, signed by the assignees, and sealed with bits of red and green paper. These too were filed and kept—some for the rest of his life. Academically, he must have been a meteor, so well informed and organized that, as his second wife Anna intimated, he may well have been a trial to his small-town teachers. For his final year of high school his parents sent him to the fee-paying grammar school in Saint John. From there, with the Parker Medal for Mathematics in hand, and the blessings of the *St. Croix Courier* ("Mr. Ganong possesses abilities of a high order"), he left for the provincial university, King's College (later the University of New Brunswick), in Fredericton in 1881.

When Charles Lyell, renowned English geologist, visited King's in 1852, he dismissed it as a nursery for classicists. He attributed this to its head, Dr. Edwin Jacob, "an old fashioned Oxonian of Corpus Christi, Oxford," and Anglican divine who disdained "practical education." Lyell, however, was unduly critical. In 1837, the college had appointed two young Scots, David Gray and James Robb, to introduce mathematics and science. Gray taught mathematics and natural philosophy but returned to Scotland after three years. Robb, however, settled and taught chemistry, biology, and geology until his early death in 1861. Robb travelled widely, and in 1849 produced the first generalized geological map of New Brunswick. The year 1840 saw the arrival of another Scot, William Brydone Jack, who taught mathematics and natural philosophy. To these he added, over the next few decades, navigation and astronomy, land surveying, and engineering. Under pressure from Lieutenant-Governor Sir Edmund Walker Head to meet the needs and expectations of a pioneer province, King's College also shed its clerical garb, converting to a secular university in 1859 and discontinuing all religious tests for students and faculty. Jack became president in 1861 and remained so throughout Ganong's residency.

Although religion had been neutralized, the classical-versus-practical argument persisted. On the proposal in 1904 for a forestry school, classicists objected to what they perceived as the university's validation of the common, the practical, and the merely useful. Ganong, by then a professor in Massachusetts, entered the debate. While no enemy of a classical education, he, like Sir Edmund Walker, insisted that the Oxford tradition in education hardly fitted the needs of a young province with a still lumber-dependent economy. "There are men at the University of New Brunswick today who could obtain a truer culture from courses properly taught in forestry than they possibly could from the Oxford type," he wrote. Years later there would be an echo of this reaction when the arts faculty of UNB's Saint John campus railed against a proposal that the subordinate college lean toward technical and vocational instruction.

Ganong was saved from an excess of classicism by James Robb's successor, a young graduate in chemistry and natural science from Harvard, Loring Woart Bailey. At Harvard, Bailey had studied with Asa Gray, the botanist; Louis Agassiz, the Swiss Pleistocene geologist;

and Josiah Parsons Cooke, the chemist. All were leaders in their fields. On arrival at King's in the fall of 1881, Ganong enrolled in the three-year course in natural science. The school had a faculty of five and an annual student enrolment of forty-five. Bailey, who was fond of saying he occupied a settee not a chair, was Ganong's chief mentor. He taught chemistry and natural sciences: zoology, botany, and geology. Chemistry passed to civil engineering in 1900, but Bailey taught geology and natural science until his retirement in 1907.

Writing to a friend in 1876, Bailey noted, without complaint, that in Fredericton he was a lone scientist; no one at the university or in the town shared his deeper interests. Even for the province, he could count only two or three people of like mind. As in Great Britain, many of the most progressive scientists were scholars with no specialized or relevant university training. Notable English examples were Humphry Davy, Michael Faraday, and Charles Darwin (who was officially a theology student at Cambridge). Bailey's closest provincial associate was George Frederic Matthew, an accomplished self-taught geologist, who was also the customs agent in Saint John; like Bailey, he was an important figure in Ganong's early life.

The son of a pharmacist, Matthew attended Saint John Grammar School twenty years before Ganong, but unlike Ganong his formal education ended there. He became a clerk with the federal treasury department that, following Confederation, was absorbed by the customs department. When Ganong asked him how a customs officer had managed to become an internationally renowned geologist and paleontologist, Matthew answered that he'd been a mineralogist first, as a boy sifting through ballast dumped in Lower Cove by lumber ships. Gneiss from the U.S. contained mica and feldspar, and lower Carboniferous limestone from the west coast of Ireland was laden with brachiopods. With Abraham Gesner's geological reports as guides, his *vade mecum*, Matthew worked over Gesner's ground on the Kennebecasis and the shore of the Bay of Fundy.

In 1857, Matthew and four other young enthusiasts founded the Steinhammer (Stonehammer) Club that in 1862, encouraged by eminent geologist J. W. Dawson, evolved into the Natural History Society of New Brunswick (NHSNB). All had read Charles Lyell's works and Gesner's provincial reports (1839–1843) and been captivated by

Gesner's collection of minerals, fossils, and rocks at the Mechanics Institute in Saint John. The Steinhammer Club's other notable member was C. F. Hartt, then a teacher at a girls' high school (Simonds) who worked with Bailey and Matthew on the geology of southern New Brunswick. With Louis Agassiz, Hartt later explored the coast and rivers of Brazil, and for a short period he was director of the department of geology in Brazil's national museum. Hartt went on to become the chair of geology at Cornell but continued his work on Brazil. He died in Rio de Janeiro in 1878.

As well as being a charter member of the Natural History Society, founded in 1862, Matthew was also its first volunteer curator. Later, he became president and, like Ganong, contributed regularly to its *Bulletin*. He worked with Loring Woart Bailey on geological mapping and the two met Sir William Logan, Dominion geologist, to discuss potential work for the Geological Survey of Canada (GSC). Like Matthew, Logan was self-taught. After Confederation, the GSC took over the mapping of New Brunswick, and among the first of Matthew's more than two hundred published papers were his reports for the GSC. He was a charter member of the Royal Society of Canada, and in 1917 he won the London Geological Society's prestigious Murchison Medal. The University of New Brunswick awarded him an LL.D., and the University of Laval a D.Sc. Other distinguished members of the society were Montague Chamberlain, author of a Maliseet dictionary and the first catalogue of Canadian birds; and George Upham Hay, who became president of the Botanical Club of Canada.

Encouraged by Professor Bailey, Ganong spent his first summer vacation scouring the shores of Passamaquoddy Bay for fossils. With his brother Edwin and UNB classmate Samuel Kain, he canoed and boated around the bay, camped on the shore, and made notes on the geology, botany, and marine life. The following summer, 1883, the NHSNB invited him to take part in its first summer camp, an archaeological/anthropological dig led by George Matthew. The objective was to examine Aboriginal kitchen middens at the mouth of the Bocabec River on the north shore of Passamaquoddy Bay. The party left Saint John by rail and at St. Stephen collected Ganong and historian-naturalist James Vroom.

Nineteen-year-old Ganong wrote field notes, and Matthew wrote a site report—published by the NHSNB's *Bulletin*—so meticulous that it is now regarded as a landmark study in North American anthropology.

Although Matthew did not describe his field techniques, they were good enough to allow him to reconstruct the Aboriginal dwellings, comment on their strategic positioning, and, from the shells and excavated animal bones, analyze their diet and their seasonal movements. As a geologist, he was also able to identify and pinpoint the locations of the rock outcrops and clay deposits from which the Aboriginals made chipped stone tools, projectile points, scrapers, and pots. Modern archaeologists bow to Matthew's conclusions but might disavow his observation that Aboriginal housekeeping did not meet his standards.

In September of the following year, 1884, the twenty-year-old Ganong embarked on his own speaking and publishing career. He read a paper (published by NHSNB in 1885) on the zoology of marine invertebrates

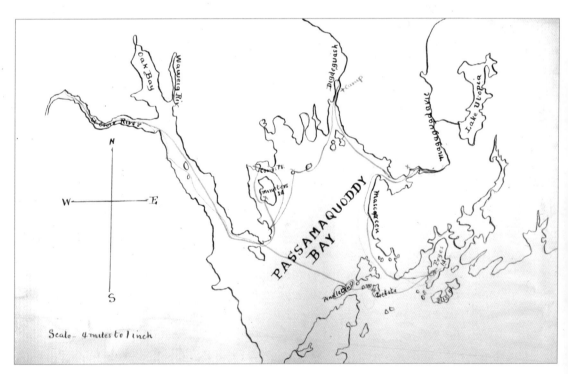

Ganong's sketch of his "down river" expedition, 1883. NEW BRUNSWICK MUSEUM, GANONG COLLECTION: F455-6A

in Passamaquoddy Bay. That summer he had been given joint charge of the management of a three-week summer field camp on Frye Island, ten kilometres from St. Andrews, and full charge of zoology and—his particular interest—the study of invertebrates. Ganong described the camp in an article for the *St. Croix Courier*: "The camp is up on a beautiful grassy slope, at the head of a hill which commands a view of all the neighbouring islands: Grand Manan, Campobello, the Wolves etc. There are four ladies present who are enjoying the delightful weather and fine scenery as well as the scientific work. The camp is under the joint management of Mr. W. F. Ganong of St. Stephen, who has charge of the dredging and marine zoology, and Mr. [G. U.] Hay who takes terrestrial and marine botany." Social life was not neglected: at night, the campers gathered around large fires, "the white tents looking very fine against the green background of trees." A room in an unoccupied house served as their laboratory.

Although he could not attend society meetings regularly, Ganong was—as George Matthew would describe him in 1914—the *Bulletin*'s "banner man," writing roughly one third of its contents. In the final paragraph of his address to mark the fiftieth anniversary of the society in November 1912, Matthew singled out Ganong: "There is no more active and energetic member of the Natural History Society of New Brunswick than Professor W. F. Ganong. He is a man who has, by his ability, energy and industry, gained a place among the scientific leaders of the United States and Canada.... He has for years spent his summer vacations in this province, exploring its mountains, forests, rivers and lakes, collecting and preserving its historical records, and publishing a vast amount of original data, much of which is embodied in our volumes of the *Bulletin*."

In a paean to the society, written in 1890 while he was at Harvard, Ganong described the society as a kind of free university for people in Saint John and southern New Brunswick. Lecturers and contributors were mostly university graduates, teachers, and professors, or—if they weren't—would have been had they been born in more recent times. None were paid. Lectures and the museum library were open to all, free of charge. Unlike many private libraries in Saint John, the NHSNB library survived the disastrous citywide fire in 1877. The society's *Bulletin* had appreciative readers and subscribers in libraries, museums, and scientific societies far beyond the borders of the province. Launched in 1882, it appeared once annually.

From 1881, the NHSNB had a ladies' auxiliary that elected its own officers and organized its own lectures in science and social science. As associate members, women could attend all the society's activities and, except for sitting on the council, participate in all public business. The society also ran a free, week-long summer school in Saint John's Market Building. Instruction took the form of lectures, laboratory work, and field excursions. At the opening session, in July 1887, George Matthew lectured on local geology, G. U. Hay on botany, Ganong on zoology, and H. C. Creed on astronomy. Later in the week, Ganong, who was then

NHSNB field party, Fredericton, 1887. Ganong is on the far right. To his right is Jean Murray Carman, his future wife, holding oars and a vasculum for plant specimens. Seated in the centre is Ganong's sister, Susan, with an improvised dredge for the collection of marine invertebrates. Samuel Kain is seated on her left. NEW BRUNSWICK MUSEUM, GANONG COLLECTION: X10987

a botany student at Harvard, lectured on sponges, corals, echinoderms, molluscs, worms, and arthropods and supervised the dissection of starfish, lobsters, and worms. Students were asked to bring a small, sharp blade, a shallow dish, a pair of needles set in wooden handles, some pins, a hand lens, a notebook, and pencils. Textbooks were not required but students were encouraged to bring any geological or zoological books they might have.

For his maiden paper to NHSNB on marine invertebrates in 1884, Ganong, as a twenty-year-old neophyte, might have submitted a catalogue—an annotated list of species and subspecies—as almost no work had been done on Passamaquoddy's invertebrates. American naturalists had combed the shores of Grand Manan and Friar's Bay, between Eastport and Campobello, but few, if any, had ventured into Passamaquoddy. Instead of an inventory, Ganong delivered a balanced lecture. He began by describing the cold waters of the bay, its habitats, and his methods of capture. In pools left by the receding tides, he used his hands to lift stones and push aside matted masses of seaweed. To collect bottom dwellers he used a dredge of his own invention: a shallow-scraping iron frame seventy-six centimetres wide attached to a rope that he dragged behind a sailboat. A fine-meshed net behind the dredge caught the disturbed material. The largest catches were molluscs, of which he found and catalogued more than fifty species. In the talk, he concentrated on the food molluscs—clams, mussels, and scallops—that were staples for the Passamaquoddy but largely ignored by Europeans. The abundant cod, pollock, and herring were caught too easily. Common squid, the best bait for cod and pollock, were also plentiful, but they were enemies of herring and if there were many of them they could prevent herring from entering the weirs. Enormous numbers of herring entered and left the bay with each tide.

For lay readers, the most engaging parts of his papers—and for readers familiar with his later published writing, the most intriguing—are the pages where he takes off his scientific hat. Later in his career he liked to describe himself as a facts man, a Gradgrind, and was careful not to do this, but at twenty he could indulge in Wordsworthian flights, the waters of Passamaquoddy Bay affecting him as strongly as (upon Wordsworth) the morning view from Westminster Bridge. "What man, if he love beauty of form could not be moved by the arrowy flight of the cuttle fish, the measured contraction and expansion of the jellyfish, the serpentine turning of the rays of the brittle star, or the beauty of motion in the rapid sweep of the arm of the barnacle." The framework of the rays of the starfish was the equal of the most delicate Grecian architecture: "grace and elegance fixed and embodied." The long, slender tentacles of the sea anemone, moving continually and decomposing the light, "send back to the eye the most varied, lovely and ever changing hues."

He was just as expansive on their medium, water, describing, as the botanist Stephen Clayden has explained, the phenomenon of biolumines-cence as probably caused by a "red tide" of microscopic algae, dinoflagel-lates, or possibly krill: "On a dark night a boat rowed over the water seems to plough through a sea of living fire; long lines of lambent flame run from the bow, while every dip of the oar makes to flash anew the ghostly gleam-ing of the water." He ended philosophically: "We study their habits and trace many secondary causes, but 'the great primary cause,' the secret of life itself, is as far from our grasp as ever, and the best we can hope to do is enter into what a great English writer calls 'the bitter Valley of Humiliation, into which only the wisest and bravest men can descend, owning themselves forever children, gathering pebbles on a boundless shore.'"

Equally uncharacteristic in the light of his later caution, were his speculations in the *University Monthly* (March 1885) on markings on flat pieces of diorite found on Minister's Island, near St. Andrews. At first sight they might have been taken for glacial striations, but on investiga-tion they were seen to have been deliberate carvings made with Native spears and axes. Most puzzling are a mesh of lines on one of the surfaces, which Ganong, without a shred of supporting evidence, interpreted as representations of Native views on life and death, and instructions about correct conduct.

Ganong graduated from UNB in the spring of 1884 with the highest honours but no declared direction. The year 1884–85 was, as the English today might say, his "gap year." That summer he tried banking, and the following fall teaching in St. Stephen, but neither appealed to him. Nor, if he carried on studying, as must have been his intention, did he want to become a narrow specialist. In his UNB notebook for 1884 he copied a long and significant passage from a lecture by Johann Gottlieb Fichte, the German philosopher: "The celebrated Fichte in his lectures on the vocation of a scholar insisted on a culture which should not be one sided, but all sided. The scholar's intellect was to expand spherically and not in a single direction only." Fichte might as well have been speaking directly to Ganong. He was proficient in every field of natural science (zoology, marine biology, geology, and botany), and although for professional reasons had narrowed his sights, he kept abreast of all of them throughout his life.

In October 1884, while contemplating his future, the American consul in St. Stephen, Paul Lange, asked Ganong if he would prepare a cabinet of the province's economic minerals for display at the World Industrial and Cotton Exposition in New Orleans. Ganong owned that he probably had enough specimens of his own to fill a cabinet, but to be representative he and Lange thought they should come from different parts of the province. In a notebook, Ganong had classified his own rocks and minerals by type—ornamental and building stones, mineral rock masses, combustible minerals, and ores—and noted the provenance of each specimen. Through the leading provincial newspapers he appealed to mine and quarry owners, listing examples of the building stones and economic minerals he wanted, adding if they would send them to St. Stephen his public-spirited father, J. H. Ganong, would pay the shipping to New Orleans. On their arrival, Ganong selected and annotated them and, ever organized, published a complete list of the exhibits and their provincial locations.

HARVARD

Early in 1885 Ganong moved to Massachusetts, where he taught natural history in classes offered free to the public by the Natural History Society of Worcester. That fall, no doubt encouraged or at least influenced by Loring Woart Bailey, he enrolled at Harvard College. Harvard then was mecca for ambitious Maritime students: Ganong reported in 1889 that sixteen of the twenty Canadian students at Harvard were from Maritime universities and all the Canadian students in the arts and humanities were Maritimers. So, too, were all the Canadian teachers on the Harvard staff. Ganong's status there isn't altogether clear; he already had a B.A. but a B.A. from a Maritime university wasn't the equivalent of a B.A. from Harvard, and all Maritime students had to catch up. Ganong enrolled as a special student in the Lawrence Scientific School, and the following year he was listed as a graduate student specializing in botany. He graduated with the class of 1888 with his second B.A., this one also *summa cum laude*. His reward was the prestigious Morgan Fellowship and appointment as assistant instructor in botany at both Harvard and its all-female coordinate institution, Radcliffe College. He became a full-time instructor in 1889. His specialty, working under Charles V. Goodale, was plant physiology: the study of the function and structure of living plants.

Except for teaching sessions at the Harvard summer school, Ganong spent his summers in New Brunswick. The year 1887 saw him back at Frye Island working with zoologists on the marine fauna. That same summer he and Samuel Kain went up the Eel River by canoe from Benton, in Carleton County, through the Chiputneticook Lakes, and down the

Perilous crossing on Grand Manan: Ganong's sketch in Samuel Kain's diary, 1888.

St. Croix to Milltown. The trip, he noted, initiated his systematic study of the physiography—the physical make-up—of the province. The summer of 1888 found him at Grand Manan with family and friends, one of whom was a Japanese visiting fellow at Harvard, Kibo Miyabe, a graduate of the University of Tokyo who taught for two years at the University of Sapporo, his alma mater. Of an earlier visit to Grand Manan, Ganong's sister Susan recalled that her brother walked the length and breadth of the island, "putting up with any fisherman available after tramping all day in search of historic and scientific data." No congenial passerby escaped his questioning. On the water he was just as active, dredging the harbour with his patent bottom scraper and sifting through the catch.

In 1889, Ganong married Jean Murray Carman—known as Muriel—the younger sister of his friend, poet Bliss Carman. The Carmans were a Loyalist family from Fredericton. While discussing arrangements with Bishop Medley for the marriage ceremony at the Anglican cathedral in Fredericton, Ganong pointedly declared his Darwinism and atheism. Medley promptly refused to marry them and extended the veto to his subordinates in the diocese, the province, and the Dominion. The Carman family, who were devout Anglicans and friends of the bishop, retreated, but Muriel, though distressed, supported Ganong. So did Bliss, who, though still a believer but also an evolutionist, consented to the union. "I should rejoice," he wrote to Muriel, "if Will could ever see his way clear to become a Christian, though I am well aware that the Christian view of the world is not one…most readily harmonized with modern science." Bliss, who was Ganong's best man, found an amenable Episcopalian church (Emmanuel) in Boston, and Ganong and Muriel were married on March 29, 1889.

Bliss Carman and Ganong were near contemporaries; they overlapped at UNB and both had worked and written for the *University Monthly*, Ganong as treasurer, Bliss as a writer. They also overlapped at Harvard, Carman studying in the English department and already making a name for himself as a poet. He contributed regularly to the *Harvard Monthly* and occasionally to the *Atlantic Monthly*, which, in March 1887, published *Low Tide on Grand Pré*, his first accomplished lyric poem. Ganong, meanwhile, had won the Morgan Medal and the guaranteed assistantship that accompanied it, and had written an original article on Jacques Cartier's exploration of the St. Lawrence. Carman and Ganong were twin stars of Harvard's Canadian contingent.

As well as preparing for his Harvard degree and instructing part-time in botany, Ganong continued to write for the *Bulletin*. His subject—New Brunswick's marine life—had no connection with his work at Harvard. The first was a paper on New Brunswick's echinoderms: the small, usually brightly coloured, hard-shelled invertebrates with a distinctive radiate or radial structure that were particularly common on the shores of the Bay of Fundy. Directed at teachers and interested naturalists, his paper was a detailed sixty-eight-page guide, published in 1886, to all the species and the available literature on them. Accompanying it were instructions on collecting, including methods of dredging, and preserving.

In November 1889 Catherine Heustis of Parrsboro, Nova Scotia, in answer to an inquiry from Ganong about starfish and other echinoderms in the Minas Basin, wrote to say how much she'd enjoyed his article and the NHSNB summer schools in general. "There is," she concluded, "a delight in the study of natural history, which nothing else on earth affords." Ganong would not have disagreed.

He followed his echinoderm paper with a monograph, published in 1889 as a book of 116 pages, on the economic molluscs of Acadia, reviving the historic use of "Acadie" to include all of the Maritime provinces. Zoologically, botanically, and geologically, the three provinces are one. Ganong made no claims for the book other than scientific accuracy, but for a twenty-four-year-old with a fresh degree in botany from Harvard, its historical and geographical reach was remarkable. The *Harvard Crimson* also thought so, recommending the publication. As well as describing edible molluscs and assessing their value and availability currently and historically, Ganong was puzzled by the differing uses (for which he had no answers except in the case of the clam) between Europe and North America. Molluscs valued in Europe were of no appeal here, and vice versa. Although abundant in Europe, clams were used only as occasional bait and there was no well-known word for them. (Champlain called them "cockles.") Here, on the other hand, clams were valued both as bait and for human consumption. By contrast the mussel, largely ignored in

North America, was considered a delicacy in Europe and irresistible hook bait for saltwater fish. In Acadia mussels were used as fertilizer; calcium-rich mussel beds, augmented by oyster shells, were dug and the mud spread on fields. In Europe, disturbing mussel beds invoked a penalty. The common starfish, however, of no economic value here, was a valued fertilizer in Europe, and sold by the wagonload to vine growers in France and farmers in Britain.

Ganong pointed out that oysters were valued on both sides of the Atlantic, but approaches to exploiting them were radically different. The French met the high demand by cultivating them, whereas the North American response was reckless and unrestrained gathering. Digging devices that cut oyster beds to pieces, pollution by riverside sawmills, and disregard of the closed season had, according to Ganong, taken the oyster to the limit of its natural productiveness. The choice facing the oyster industry of Acadia was free fishing and a lingering death, or vigorous government intervention and lasting prosperity. He advised that beds be harvested no more than once every three years, the closed season enforced, digging devices restricted, and mills prevented from dumping sawdust. He also thought that cultivated beds should be protected and, as if to anticipate the demands of modern fish farmers, that the culturists should be accorded the same rights and protection as farmers on land. Ganong's recommendations were quoted in full by the Department of Fisheries in its annual report for 1889.

In New Brunswick the oyster industry was confined to the east coast where the waters are shallow and relatively warm and the tides slight; summer temperatures in the turbulent Bay of Fundy are too cold for breeding and large starfish, the oyster's worst enemy, were abundant. The wash of the heavy Fundy tides would also cover the living molluscs with silt, inhibiting their growth. In an 1898 report for the *Bulletin*, Ganong described how his uncle G. W. Ganong had emptied two barrels of live oysters from the Gulf of St. Lawrence and several barrels of oyster shells into shallow water at Oak Bay, an arm of Passamaquoddy Bay, where he had a summer cottage. The oysters perished. Ganong had dredged the bottom of Oak Bay several times at the point where the oysters had been introduced but brought up only dead shells and seaweed that showed no trace of young. He made the report so that no future naturalist would mistake the shells as evidence of the recent natural occurrence of oysters in the bay.

Ganong ended his 1889 monograph on the economic molluscs with a reference to the dreaded *Teredo navalis*, a wood-eating worm that in the shallower, warmer waters of the North Shore could quickly destroy wharves, docks, and wooden vessels. Ship bottoms could be protected with copper sheathing and wharves and docks with creosote. In Japan, according to his friend Miyabe, several coats of lacquering had the same effect. In the turbid, colder waters of the Bay of Fundy the Teredo was less of a scourge, but Ganong knew of a broad and strong tide-dam in Passamaquoddy that had been destroyed by the worm within the space of six years. In Saint John Harbour, however, the Teredo, according to Samuel Kain, was not a threat, the consensus being its dislike of great volumes of fresh water.

MUNICH

Ganong was no careerist, but monographs and articles on marine zoology and marine culture, however well regarded, would not advance his career as a botanist. So, in early June 1893, along with 593 American students, he and his wife, Muriel, set out on the postgraduate trail to Munich, Germany; Muriel to continue her studies of modern languages, he to get a Ph.D. Seen off by Bliss Carman, they sailed from New York.

In the 1890s, American academics, and scientists in particular, bowed before the acclaimed rigour of German research. In his 1865 report on higher education in Germany for an English schools commission, Matthew Arnold lighted upon the emphasis given to science and the need for English schools and colleges to follow the German lead: "The French university has no liberty, and the English universities have no science; the German universities have both." The most coveted prize was a German doctorate: the Holy Grail that opened doors to American university departments.

In the second half of the nineteenth century, German naturalists changed direction. Previous approaches had been "philosophical" (Hegelian), based on theory, and the overarching ideas that researchers were required to substantiate with supporting evidence. It was a case of theory first, supporting facts later. By the middle of the century, however, the "painstaking investigation of particulars" as the historian L. R. Veysey put it, had replaced inspirational theorizing. The sea change, the so-called inductive approach, owed much to Alexander von Humboldt, the great naturalist who, on his return to Germany from South America in 1827, insisted upon hands-on, empirical studies of plants, soils, relief, and drainage. "Facts endure," he wrote, when philosophic structures have long crumbled. There was to be no more "moony philosophizing." In the wrong hands—and there were a number of these—the emphasis on facts resulted in draconian Gradgrindism and the destruction of imagination. Thomas Chamberlin, an American geologist–geographer and a devout convert to the new faith, framed the gospel: "Facts and rigorous inductions from facts displace all preconceptions....If need be, previous intellectual affectations are crushed without remorse. Facts take their place before reasoning and before ideals, however [he added regrettably] beautiful and lofty these may seem." American scientists, thirsting for a new faith, rushed to the altar. The philosopher Josiah Royce, who was no disciple of the new science, acknowledged the single-minded devotion of his compatriots: "England was passed by. It was understood to be not scholarly enough. France, too, was then neglected. German scholarship was our master and our guide."

Ganong's destination was the University of Munich where Karl Ritter von Goebel, his adviser there, had created a botanical garden and founded a botanical institute. In 1893 it was a centre for the study of plant morphology, the physical form and external structure of plants, as distinct from plant anatomy, the study of their internal structure, especially at the microscopic level. To distance himself from earlier schools of botany that regarded the physical form of plants as variants or expressions of an ideal, von Goebel travelled widely to examine plants in their natural settings. His legacy to plant morphology was a three-volume work he called *Organography* to avoid any association with idealistic morphology. By questioning why plants took the form they did, where they did, he founded the study of plant morphology and advanced that of plant geography. In an address on adaptive phenomena in plants, at the Munich Academy of Sciences in 1898, he declared the next stage in botany would focus upon the relationship of plants to the external world. Taxonomy, the classification and description of plants, was outmoded. Asa Gray, the pioneer of botany at Harvard and himself a classifier and taxonomist, recognized the value of the German approach. Science had become experimental and most Americans were convinced that only in Germany could they gain the grounding they sought.

At Munich, Ganong chose cacti as his research subject. There is no evidence to suggest he had ever been to a desert or dryland region, and would have seen cacti only in greenhouses. The Harvard Herbarium, which collected plants from all over the globe, was then the centre for botanical research in the U.S. Ganong completed his dissertation, "Contributions to the Knowledge of the Morphology and Biology of Cacti," in July 1894, the year following his arrival. The average time for completion of the degree was three years. He also wrote the dissertation, and presumably defended it, in German, which indicates a good deal of advance work at Harvard on both the thesis and the language. His subject was the special adaptations of cacti to extremes of heat and aridity, a problem introduced by von Goebel in an earlier publication. The following year he published, in English, a modified version of his dissertation in the *Botanical Gazette*, outlining the great need for extended field studies. Not even von Goebel in Venezuela had been able to give more than cursory attention to desert conditions. Until there were year-round studies of rainfall, dew formation, soil conditions, winds, and daily and seasonal variations in temperature, we could only guess at the adaptations made by desert and dryland plants.

Back in America, Ganong continued his work on cacti and in 1898 he published his findings as a long article in the *Annals of Botany*. His objective had been to discover the extent to which the distinctive morphological features of the adult plants were present in the embryos and at what stages they develop. No comparative study of the young stages in cacti had ever been attempted. Ganong began by gathering reliably identified seeds collected by qualified field botanists in Arizona and Southern California and gardens in Jamaica, Palermo, and Florence. He planted these in a New England greenhouse. Controlled conditions in a northern greenhouse were not, he insisted, qualitatively different from conditions in the field at home. Germination in deserts and drylands occurs in the cloudy, rainy season, a condition that could be replicated in a northern greenhouse. Ganong had found greenhouse embryos did not grow well if exposed to bright light. Soil conditions seemed to have little effect on growth; embryos of the same species sown in sand, peat, and sawdust were not appreciably different from one another. While he conceded his study would have been more convincing if conducted at a desert or dryland station, he did not think the removal of the seeds to his New England plant laboratory invalidated his observations. He would, however, express delight at the Carnegie Institution's support for the building of America's first desert botanical laboratory on an 860-acre site just west of Tucson, Arizona, in 1902–03.

From his study of a number of separate species, Ganong concluded that adaptive changes in the size and form of the embryos are preceded by such changes in the adults, not vice versa. This was contrary to expectations and counterintuitive. In contrast to the development of individual plants, the long-term evolutionary changes in morphology appeared to arise in reverse order, the adult shaping the embryo and the embryo the seed. As the size of the adult plants diminished in response to the increasing dryness of their habitats, so then did the size of the embryos and seeds. In the case of *Phyllocactus*, Ganong demonstrated that flattening in the epicotyl (the shoot arising from the germinating seed, below the first leaves) likewise worked backward from the adult, not forward from the embryo. A new character, first selected for its adaptive benefit to the adult stages of the plant, works its way back over countless generations to the earliest stages of the seedling, ultimately replacing the ancestral characters, which then cease to be repeated.

He found that the same principle, although different in detail, applied to all the species: that the "ground form of the embryos is imposed by the ground form of the adults." He concluded: "Taking the family as a whole, we may picture successive waves…of characters acquired by adaptation in the adults sweeping back into the later seedlings, and wiping out earlier characters."

To end the article he drew a phylogenetic tree, the first for the *Cactaceae*. By combining his own studies of the morphology of cactus embryos and seedlings with data from other researchers, he was able to show the various genera of the cactus family and the probable evolutionary relations between them. The ancestral form is in the tree trunk, and its descendants are in the branches, which also show the relative times of their origin and the distances between them. In the diagram, the *Persekia*, on the far left, is nearest to the original stem form of the family; the *Opuntia* is derived from it and the two of them, still existing, form a single axial branch.

The originality of Ganong's thesis—that the working back of the adult stage to the epicotyl and finally to the embryos and the seeds as the

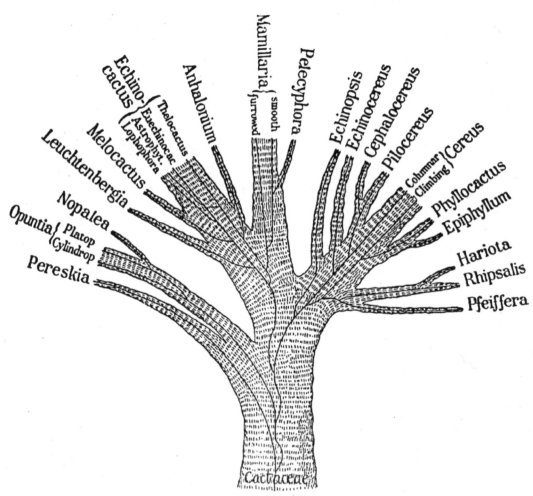

Ganong's Phylogenetic Tree showing the probable evolutionary relationships between various genera of the cactus family.

climate became drier—was an adaptive strategy first acknowledged in print in 1910 by Ethel de Fraine, a botanist working at the University of London. More recently, a small group of botanists working at universities in Canada (Saskatchewan) and Brazil added a warm note of approval. In a 2013 paper they emphasized the importance of seedling morphology in vegetation studies and pointed out that the vast majority of studies dealing with the seedlings of cacti have focused on the role of nursing plants and the biotic and abiotic factors in the survival of offspring. As a result, the morphology and anatomy and the initial stages of plantlets of *Cactaceae*, regrettably, remain largely unexplored. Ganong's century-old dissertation and article, they acknowledge, was the pioneer study that pointed the way.

His year in Germany is a black hole in the voluminous Ganong Archive. For a man who never seemed to stop writing when at home, his silence on the German interlude is puzzling. Not a single personal letter from Ganong, or from his wife, has found its way into the Ganong Archive in the New Brunswick Museum. On his return, he admitted to having been mighty homesick. His response to this distress seems to have been silence. The only surviving observations on his German experience are two commentaries on German education, one to the NHSNB and the other to the *Educational Review*. While in Germany, Ganong also managed to write an article for the *Bulletin* on phytobiology, his word for the relationship between plants and their environs, and he encouraged its pursuit by local botanists. Taxonomy had become too complicated, and once local plants had been identified, further research required travel.

Ganong's reward for his German venture was a Ph.D. and a passport to an academic career. In other ways, though, it seems to have been a trial. German university buildings were generally austere, and contemporary reports made no reference to collegial life. German students attended classes and laboratories, lived in rooms, and ate with their landladies or at inns. There was no college life, no common rooms, and no common dining halls. The university, as one of the officers proclaimed, "keeps no boarding house." Even for undergraduates, attendance at lectures was voluntary, and research students could decide when to take the final comprehensive exam. They could also move freely between universities.

1893

In Europe

Walk in Tirol and Switzerland

1894

In Europe.

~~Walk~~

Munich and England.

Mighty homesick for N. B.

Ganong's pointed "Mighty homesick for N. B." journal entry, 1893–94. New Brunswick Museum, Ganong Collection: F455-23 (A & B)

In his entry for the 1912 Harvard yearbook, Ganong noted that he had spent some time at the University of Bonn while in Germany, but there is no other record of this. The freedom, if not the lack of collegiality, undoubtedly suited Ganong, the most self-directed of scholars. His mentor von Goebel was a mere advisor.

In the summer of 1893, shortly after arriving in Europe, Ganong went on a month-long walking tour through the Tyrol to Interlaken in some of the most beautiful parts of southern Germany, Austria, and Switzerland. His companion was George F. Pierce, a botanist and fellow graduate student at Munich and Ganong's assistant at Harvard and Radcliffe. It was a gentleman's tour: they followed the roads, carried umbrellas instead of walking sticks, did no mountain climbing or glacier work, and put up at wayside inns.

The Tyrol is one of the most beautiful parts of the Alps, combining spectacular Alpine scenery with—in the valleys and on the flat shoulders above the valley floors—picturesque villages and farms: a naturalist's and cultural geographer's delight. Ganong, however, seems to have been unmoved, remarking only on the disturbing human imprint on the landscape. For Ganong, as for Omar Khayyam, wilderness was paradise enough. When abroad, he appears to have been the kind of irksome traveller who compared everything, usually unfavourably, with home. On his return to New Brunswick he told his sister, Susan, that he judged all German rivers in terms of their suitability for canoeing, even the famed Gorge of the Rhine. None measured up.

He never returned to Europe.

Years later he repeated, with obvious approval, the sentiments of a Northampton acquaintance who, when asked which part of his European journey he enjoyed most, replied, "the part from New York back to Northampton." Ganong could be just as dismissive when New Brunswick was the counter attraction. When asked by his mother and sister how he would pass the time while waiting for the return of his second wife, Anna Hobbet, from the West to Rothesay in the summer of 1925, he replied, "I will spend the time [taking] trips by auto from Rothesay to places more alluring than Banff, Lake Louise, the Riviera *et al* combined." Ganong's first wife, Jean Murray Carman, died in 1920.

Nor at the University of Munich was Ganong greatly impressed with the vaunted German research methods. In a letter read before NHSNB in Saint John he wrote: "I have been saved a disappointment at the outset by not expecting to find a great illuminating German 'method' for I have long been convinced that the only method of preeminent value is the true education of the individual." Only excerpts from that letter, published in the *Educational Review* in 1895, have survived, so what precisely he meant by the "true education" of the individual isn't clear. Elsewhere in the letter he indicated that the general principle at German universities was to provide the means for research and study rather than to teach. There was far less method than in America. German discipline in study and work in general he attributed, with no apparent fear that this might have unfortunate consequences, to that country's policy of mandatory military service upon graduation after high school. In investigation, one of its manifestations was a taste for the encyclopaedic: the disciplined, sometimes laborious amassing of facts useful in themselves and indispensable as a basis for theory. Ganong was not unaffected by this. He may not have been impressed by the German method, but exposure to it may well have reined in his imagination. After his sojourn in Munich, he made fewer flights of fancy and few concessions to poetic truths, in print at least. Facts and exactitude ruled.

For Ganong, a lesson more valuable than anything German scholarship could offer was the German devotion to work and community. However humble the trade, Germans stuck undeviatingly to it, seldom changing their occupations. Trades and professions provided a livelihood, but first and foremost served the community. "A man's ideal relationship to his community," Ganong wrote, "is not to make his living from it, but to do it the greatest possible service." He cited the example of an elderly schoolmaster he met in the Tyrol who had given his life to teaching peasant children. With earnings smaller than those of a schoolteacher in rural New Brunswick, he had filled his small house with apparatus—both homemade and bought—for teaching physics, astronomy, and natural history. Twenty years later, Ganong hadn't changed his mind about public service. In a letter to G. U. Hay, president of the NHSNB, on the occasion of the Society's fiftieth anniversary, he wrote that he looked forward to the day "when scientific and learned societies and their leaders will take a much more prominent part in public affairs." He added that in New Brunswick, thanks to the work of the NHSNB, ("an admirably managed scientific society wholly devoted to the interests of the province"), the ground had been well prepared.

On leaving Munich, Ganong's duty as a scholar and a scientist was clear. The academic ladder, networking, and office seeking would take a back seat. He would broadcast his findings to as wide an audience as possible. The corollary of this was that as an investigator he would tap the resources of the community, encourage local studies, and make use of local knowledge. Whereas his academic colleagues might dismiss or disdain the uneducated, Ganong believed that, with encouragement and direction, they could become reliable investigators. A local source was as important to him as an academic one. For a 1900 issue of the *Educational Review*, he wrote a five-page article on suggestions for the investigation of local history, indicating how this might be done. He issued a similar challenge to naturalists in his paper "Upon biological opportunity in New Brunswick" for an 1899 issue (no. 17) of the *Bulletin*.

Ganong also embraced local historians. He persuaded James Vroom, the gifted but modest St. Stephen town clerk and treasurer who was also an accomplished naturalist, to publish a history of Charlotte County. It was serialized in the *St. Croix Courier*. In 1928, near the end of his long and distinguished academic career, Ganong also urged J. E. Humphreys, a local historian from Petitcodiac, to write a history of Westmorland County, or at least the part of it he knew best. Ganong had been so impressed by notes and historical material sent to him that in a series of letters he outlined how a history might be approached. He supplied a list of possible chapter headings and offered to draw maps to illustrate the text. "If only you would begin," wrote Ganong, "I would…read over your MS. chapters as prepared, and make any suggestions I could, [appending] additional facts if I have any….And I can assure you that there would be <u>no delay</u> in this case as I would read and return everything immediately…. I am hoping very much indeed that you will do this. I could perhaps supply some notes here and there, or brief sketches of the scientific features of the region, and…draw you a map for publication…. It would be a pleasure for me to do this…and [I] will feel it a very great loss if you don't."

His encouragement and offers to help astounded Humphreys, the owner of a builders' supply business in Petitcodiac. As an historian, he was unpublished and unknown. Toward the end of their long association, which embraced visits as well as letters from Ganong, he wrote: "Realizing the magnitude of the work you are engaged in, and how busy you must be, your kind offer touched me very much. All along I have been fully conscious of my need of help and I believe if it had not been for the help you have given me in the past, by your suggestions, books and maps, I would have become discouraged and dropped the work. ... I have often thought of...telling you of my deep appreciation of your kindness and courtesy in taking so much of your time and giving me so much information and so many of your published transactions. I prize every letter and pamphlet received from you and have carefully preserved them."

Ganong was that rarity, a scholar of extraordinary range and depth who was also the people's mentor.

Chapter 2

———— ❧❧ ❧❧ ————

SMITH COLLEGE

E ven before he returned to America from Germany in the summer
of 1896, an academic door opened for Ganong. Smith College in
Northampton, Massachusetts, needed a professor of botany and
a director for its botanic garden. Smith offered and Ganong accepted.
Smith is a women's college, founded in 1875, and its president, L. Clark
Seelye, aimed to strengthen the life sciences, botany among them. In the
spring of 1894 he approached George Lincoln Goodale, Professor of
Botany at Harvard and Ganong's former mentor and supervisor. Goodale
provided a short list of suitable candidates with Ganong's name at the top.
In a letter to Munich, he advised Ganong to accept any offer from Seelye
as there would be no openings at Harvard for several years. With faith
in Goodale's judgement but little in the value of German Ph.D.s, Seelye
offered Ganong the position, adding that his appointment would not be
conditional on the completion of his degree. For skeptical Americans,
German universities were "diploma mills" and speedily obtained Ph.D.s
were merely specious labels designed to impress. Seelye did suggest,
however, that it might reassure the trustees if Ganong returned with
one in hand. Ganong did, and he taught at Smith for thirty-two years,
all the while retaining his Canadian citizenship. In June of that year,

Bliss Carman, then living in Cambridge, Massachusetts, attended Smith's graduation exercises and gave a reading at their "Class Day '94." After the ceremonies he wrote to his sister, Muriel, saying he liked the atmosphere there very much. "They are all earnest and simple and unhurried by the modern curse of decadence (speed)."

To landscape the grounds at Smith, Seelye hired the Brookline, Massachusetts, firm of Olmsted, Olmsted, and Eliot. Frederick Law Olmsted, the senior partner, had designed Central Park in New York and the Boston park system, and the company had landscaped the campuses of a number of colleges in the east (among them Amherst, Mount Holyoke, and the Massachusetts Agricultural College) and the Midwest. Seelye's mandate was a design in the naturalistic English Romantic style.

The Systemics Garden, Paradise Pond, and Herbaceous Garden on the Smith College grounds. SMITH COLLEGE ARCHIVES: DB41

When travelling in Europe he had been impressed by the use of gardens, both as ornaments and as teaching aids in schools, colleges, and public places. His ambition was to make an arboretum of the thirty-acre campus—an attractive yet instructive landscape of grouped trees and shrubs. Seelye and the Olmsteds divided the grounds into unfenced sections, each devoted to a single family of woody plants and arranged according to a system devised by George Bentham and Joseph Dalton Hooker, both English taxonomists associated with Kew Gardens, London.

By 1894, the year of Ganong's appointment, Olmsted, Olmsted, and Eliot had completed their design and begun planting. The design called for a picturesque arrangement of curving drives, walkways, ponds, and artfully planted trees and shrubs. For Ganong, as he explained in the *Smith College Monthly* in 1895, the challenge was to combine aesthetics and science, successfully achieved in places like Pisa and Padua, Italy, but never before attempted in the United States.

Botany had been offered at Smith from the outset, but not established as a separate department until 1890. A science building, Lily Hall, built in 1886, housed both the botany and biology departments; it was one of the first science buildings in America built exclusively for women. As a subject for young women in the mid- to late nineteenth century, botany held certain advantages over zoology; it did not require the dissection of animals, and the sexual functions of plants were discreet. Horticulture and ornamental gardening had also, since the Middle Ages, been regarded as a woman's domain. Flowers and herbs were indispensable in the kitchen and apothecary, and in the absence of chemical deodorizers they were used to sweeten and decorate living quarters. When it had been a science of recognition and classification, botany was not difficult and appealed to both sexes. Women were encouraged to study it even though few women went on to become professional botanists. In the first published survey of American botanists in 1873, 13 percent of the 599 named botanists were women; by 1878 the proportion had risen to 16 percent of 982. Seelye and Ganong were determined not only to remove gender barriers in scientific study but to avoid what Ganong called "utilitophobia" in the curricula of liberal arts colleges; that is, the objection to any course of study simply because it happened to be useful.

With funds donated by the Lymans, a prominent Northampton family, Seelye and Ganong replaced an existing small greenhouse with a tall palm house, replete with an iron filigree roof, modelled after the Palm House at Kew Gardens in London. Adjoining the palm house were a number of smaller rectangular rooms, each simulating one of the earth's major climates. The Tropical Room featured smaller tropical plants; the Palm House, tall tree ferns, palms, bamboo, fig and banana trees; the Acacia and Cactus Room, plants of desert and dry climates; and the Cool and Warm Temperate Rooms, plants from the humid middle climatic zones. Ganong and Seelye hired Edward J. Canning as head gardener; he had trained at Kew Gardens and Beaver Castle in England and worked for six years in private gardens and nurseries in America.

Smith College acquired its exotic plants by purchase or exchange from greenhouses in all parts of the world, some as close as the Arnold Arboretum at Harvard and others as distant as the Royal Botanic Garden in Java, or the University of Tokyo in Japan. Ganong kept a ledger book of plants and seeds obtained from other institutions. In addition to the rooms set aside for specific climates, there was an Experiment Room where seniors in plant physiology could work through series of experiments in plant nutrition, growth, and irritability, the manner by which plants, from the time they leave the seed, guide their growing parts in the most advantageous directions. Adjacent to the Plant House was an herbaceous garden where plants could be grown and monitored in small plots. In addition to it was a pond well stocked with water plants, a bog for marsh forms, and a rockery for alpine and dryland plants. There were additions to the Plant House in 1902, and in 1904, with more funds from the Lymans, brick replaced the original wood.

Two years after his appointment, in December 1897, Ganong wrote an article for *Garden and Forest*, a weekly journal launched by Charles Sprague, the founding director of the Arnold Arboretum at Harvard, outlining the role of a college greenhouse and botanic garden. For proponents of hands-on, empirical botany, a botanic garden and a partitioned greenhouse were indispensable. If Lyman House seemed overly large, Ganong asked visitors to keep in mind the nature of the liberal college year. There were few graduate students, no summer school or summer term, and the greenhouses allowed for the year-round growth—and study through the fall and winter—of plants that would otherwise be dormant or dead.

In an article on the same subject, written fifteen years later for *Science*, Ganong reiterated the importance of greenhouses. Of all the teaching aids in botany, he wrote, they were by far the most important and he admitted to being extremely pleased with his own planned arrangement. Least useful, because of the long summer vacation, was the herbaceous garden of seasonal plants that died in the fall when the students returned to college. For it, he was making a particular effort to obtain plants that bloom in the spring or autumn, even though he insisted the bloom was not always the most important part of a plant, nor the study of flowers the most essential part of botany. In most cases, the vegetative parts were of as much use in spring and autumn as in summer.

In the wider garden, there could be no reservations about the collection of trees and shrubs. They were in condition for study earlier in the

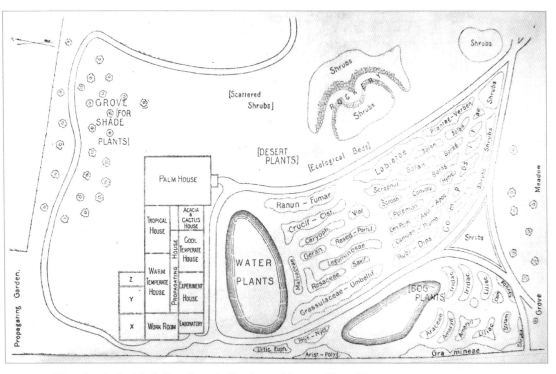

Plans for the Smith College Botanic Garden and Lyman Plant House. NEW BRUNSWICK MUSEUM, GANONG COLLECTION: F448-33

spring and later in the fall than herbaceous plants, and they could even be studied during the winter when herbaceous plants were not visible at all. While emphasizing that Smith's gardens were primarily for instruction, he conceded that arrangements of plants that evoked attention and admiration were useful teaching aids, instruction being more effective when subjects pleased the eye. An attractive campus too, he added, loosened the purse strings of parents, alumni, and benefactors. He also pointed to the social advantages of his greenhouses: they were comfortable venues for winter visitations.

The one problem, which he shared with directors of botanic gardens throughout the world—and for which he had no satisfactory solution—was devising a system of labelling that didn't overwhelm casual visitors or botany students. Gardens and greenhouses were valuable educationally only to the extent that labels fully indicated the scientific and common names of each plant as well as its family and native home. How to convey this information concisely and effectively in one label was a problem yet to be resolved. On the question of campus-wide appreciation of the gardens and greenhouses, Ganong promised to post occasional bulletins in the Halls announcing the blooming of particular plants and other phenomena that might be of general interest.

At Smith, Ganong not only planned his own greenhouses and laboratories, but also wrote his own texts and instructional books. There was no shortage of books in what has been dubbed the Golden Age of Botany, but because approaches to plants had changed from taxonomy and classification to plant physiology (the study of process and function) and plant relations to their environments, Ganong felt it was time for new texts. He also thought it was time for a renewed commitment to the teaching of botany. The first official recognition of the need came in 1900 when the Society for Plant Morphology and Physiology appointed a three-man committee (W. F. Ganong, F. E. Lloyd, and the noted ecologist Henry C. Cowles) to formulate a high school course in botany that would satisfy college and university entry requirements. The committee sat for six years before the Botanical Society of America took over.

The first of Ganong's books, *The Teaching Botanist*, appeared in 1899; the second, *A Laboratory Course in Plant Physiology*, in 1901; the third,

The Living Plant, in 1913; and the fourth, *A Textbook of Botany for Colleges*, in 1920. *A Laboratory Course in Plant Physiology* was enlarged, entirely rewritten, and republished in 1908. The others were also revised and reprinted over time. The books were intended as guides for students and teachers of botany, not the research-oriented. Raymond J. Pool, Professor of Botany at the University of Nebraska in 1921, wrote to Ganong to tell him that his department so admired his *Textbook of Botany* it had discarded all others. In future editions, Pool suggested, a short chapter on plant cells and tissues written in Ganong's "excellent style" would improve the "teachability" of the text, which was being used in the College of Agriculture as well as in the College of Arts and Science. There was also high praise from the *Botanical Gazette*. It considered his book on laboratory practices in plant physiology to be the best in any language. "The style is clear, vivid and scholarly throughout. We can think of no book yet published which might better serve as a guide to the acquisition of a general physiological education."

The Lyman Plant House at Smith College. SMITH COLLEGE ARCHIVES: DB3002

C. Stuart Gager of the Brooklyn Botanic Garden urged teachers to memorize and take to heart the first chapter of the revised ("rewritten almost throughout") second edition of *The Teaching Botanist*, released in 1910. Progressive teachers would already possess well-worn copies of the decade-old first edition that Gager described as a pioneer contribution to the pedagogy of their subject. "Teachers of all grades, experienced and inexperienced," he wrote of the second edition, "cannot fail to derive both profit and inspiration from this admirable volume." While taking issue with some of Ganong's conclusions in *The Living Plant*, Gager regarded the book as unique, being the only attempt as far as he knew to popularize the entire range of plant physiology. For readers who might think this an elementary exercise, he issued the caveat that only a gifted teacher and researcher who was also an accomplished writer would undertake it. Botany might, in a sense, be regarded as a popular science but its popularity, he cautioned, "diminishes approximately as the square of the distance from the 'how-to-know-the-wild flowers' phase of it."

In 1938, six years after Ganong's retirement, Professor Burton E. Livingston, a distinguished professor of plant physiology at Johns Hopkins University, wrote Ganong to congratulate him on his election as a lifelong emeritus to the Association of Plant Physiologists and, more importantly, to tell him of the enduring worth of his botanical writings. "As the years go by and you look back upon your lasting work in botany and plant physiology," he wrote, "I hope you get a little pleasure from the lasting excellence of that book of yours *The Living Plant*. When we discuss the art of literary presentation I have long been telling our graduate students to study that book as a fine example, and I am still continuing in that advice. They need examples of attractive and readable presentation that is at the same time truthful and there are few such examples. Your book is the best I know of and we do not forget your service to the science!"

Possibly the most satisfying praise came from curious lay readers, the audience Ganong was always trying to reach. C. A. Weatherby of Connecticut—a self-taught botanist who would become senior curator of Harvard's Gray Herbarium—encouraged by the "warm relation" Ganong had established with readers through the simply and beautifully written

a several-metres-thick mass of interlaced air-storing sedges and peat moss separated from the underlying marsh mud by a half-metre of water.

The marshes and the Fundy lowlands were first settled in the seventeenth century by *saulniers* or marsh workers from the shallow estuaries of the Charente and the Garonne in the Saintonge district of western France. In France they built dykes to trap salt water and, by allowing the water to evaporate, make salt. On the Bay of Fundy they reversed the process, building dykes to keep the salt water out, and then sluices to drain rainwater from the marshlands and flush out the salt. The first step was to build a dyke or levee from a frame of solid tree trunks, interlaced with branches and saplings, roughly ten to twelve feet wide at the base and tapering toward the top. The space between the trunks they filled with mud and tamped clay, and to prevent infiltration by sea water they covered the outer walls with a layer of carefully fitted sod. To drain the marshes behind the dykes they dug ditches and canals directed toward *aboiteaux*, long, rectangular sluice boxes of tamarack plank, roughly a half-metre square and up to six metres long, at the base of the dykes. At low tide, a hinged valve or clapper at the seaward end of the sluices allowed rainwater to escape, but it closed when subjected to pressure from the opposite direction. Rainwater drainage through the clapper valves, in two to three years, reduced the salinity of the soil behind the dykes.

After the settlement there were two distinct environments: reclaimed marshland kept largely free of salt by the drainage ditches and *aboiteaux*, and freshwater bogs and lakes farther inland beyond the reach of salt water. Early in the nineteenth century, these too were reclaimed—through a process that Ganong thought unique—by digging canals to the tidal rivers, draining the fresh water, and replacing it with tidal sea water that killed the freshwater plants and at the same time deposited rich marsh mud.

From the standpoint of botanical diversity the plants themselves were not exceptional, but they were important ecologically because of the adaptations they made to survive in an environment subjected periodically to dramatic interchanges of fresh and salt water. On the dyked marshes the dominant species were tall, dense timothy and couch grasses, both introduced from Europe. Timothy dominated on the higher, older, salt-free parts, but both types grew side by side. No native species could compete. Marsh soils were productive, maintaining their fertility, sometimes for decades, without fertilizers and with no cultivation beyond an occasional plowing when a single crop of oats was sown. But because they were fine, dense, and poorly aerated they were not equally good for all crops. Shallow rooted English hay grasses and grains did well on them, but root crops had difficulty penetrating the dense soils.

To restore fertility after many years of continuous haying, the dykes were broken, and for two or three years muddy sea water was allowed to flow freely over the old marsh. "Tiding" or "letting the tide on the marsh" killed most or all of the existing vegetation and led to the deposit of new mud. Broadleaf bog plants, bushes, and timothy were often killed by a single tide, turning white or brown and, in the case of the bushes, black "as if scorched by fire." Ganong attributed the lethality, tentatively, to salt damage to the protoplasm and the root hairs, impairing the ability of the latter to absorb water. Tiding continued for two or three years until several inches of mud had been laid down, then the dykes were rebuilt, the drains opened, and the marsh left to itself to desalinate. The struggle with fresh water, however, was incessant. Poor drainage allowed bog plants and poorer hays to replace the more valuable varieties. Failure to drain could end with takeover by then unusable spagnum mosses and bog plants. On the well-drained areas, vegetation went through a series of changes that ended with the restoration of the grasses, first by the more salt-tolerant couch grasses and then, within four or five years, by timothy; all without any aid beyond keeping the drains in order. The marshes, noted Ganong, offered a grand opportunity to study the nature of plant competition and succession.

Though hailed by Cowles and Kohler as a classic study in ecology, Ganong had no illusions about the series' limitations. The only parts that satisfied were his detailed descriptions of plants and of the ways in which they were grouped, even though these observations, as in most ecological studies, were restricted to summer. Without time and adequate equipment he had not added to existing knowledge of marshland soils and climate, or to the physiology of marshland plants. While he had been able to point to general ways in which plants compete and cooperate to form communities he, like other botanists, knew little of the detailed mechanisms. In a broad way, he continued, we can often see how one plant can dominate another: how, for example, a shade-loving plant can oust a sun-loving one or how mineral exhaustion in a soil might damage one plant and favour another, but we do not know precisely what, quoting the Danish pioneer ecologist Eugenius Warming, "the weapons are with which plants force one another from their positions." Ignorance on virtually all these fronts explained why writing on ecology, including his own, contained so much qualification. Crutch words or phrases such as "probably," "doubtless," and "in a general way" salted most texts. Ganong insisted the answer to Warming's and other questions—on which any significant advance in plant ecology depended—could be provided only by trained investigators, equipped with field laboratories, stationed for months or years, winter and summer, at the places to be investigated.

Even though, lacking field equipment and time, Ganong had not addressed the physiology of marshland plants, in the matter of marshland soils he had not been as lax as he inferred. In August 1898 he collected samples of five marshland soils: two top soils, two underlying clays within reach of plant roots, and a freshly laid mud. He sent these to F. T. Shutt, the chemist at the Dominion Experimental Farm in Ottawa, for analysis. Ganong's objectives were both scientific and economic: he was curious about the physical structure and chemical nature of the soils, but he also wanted to match soils with productivity and correct any chemical or structural deficiencies. While soils in low-lying places might benefit from applications of fertilizer, lime, organic manure, better drainage, and occasional cultivation, well drained and well aerated soils in slightly more elevated hay lands had been cropped for forty years without plowing, fertilizing, tiding, or any other treatment. Although some of the soils were not rich in elements essential to fertility, such as nitrogen, potash, and phosphorous, they were in a form that could readily be used by crops. Common salt in the soils might be of no direct benefit to plants, but it served to liberate inert or locked-up nutrients. However, too frequent use of salt muds ("mudding") without the addition of manures would in time impoverish the soil, removing the humus that would have to be replaced by barnyard or other organic manure. In short, marsh mud needed to be applied judiciously. "Too many [practitioners]," Shutt's report concluded, "have erred in its indiscriminate application, under the impression that it was a complete fertilizer, and could be used in any quantity without endangering the soil." In spite of the limitations of the soils, George Warren, a drainage engineer with the U.S. Department of Agriculture, after his tour of the Fundy marshlands in November 1910, could write as follows to Ganong. He exclaimed that reclaimed marshland soils at the head of the Bay of Fundy—a region of sparse population and relatively poor markets—would easily be worth six to eight times as much per acre as (presumably unimproved) marshland soils on the Atlantic coast within a few hours' ride of cities of 700,000 or more.

THE RAISED PEAT BOGS OF
CHARLOTTE AND SAINT JOHN COUNTIES

The Fundy bogs and marshes were not Ganong's first encounter with saturated lands. In the summer of 1890, when he was still at Harvard, a local naturalist, C. E. Boardman from St. Stephen, invited him to visit a peat bog whose centre stood many feet higher than its margins. Questioning such a bog's very existence, Ganong canvassed his botanical colleagues. Years earlier one of them had seen a reference in a botanical journal to a raised peat bog (*hochmoor*) in Sweden, but the others were as skeptical as Ganong. On seeing the bog, however, near Seely's Cove about forty-eight kilometres east of St. Stephen, his doubts were dispelled. His account of the visit, in the May 1891 issue of the *Botanical Gazette*, and subsequent articles on Bay of Fundy and North Shore bogs in *Transactions* and the *Bulletin*, provided the first descriptions of raised peat bogs in North America.

About 1 kilometre long and 182 metres wide, the Seely's Cove bog rose dome-like about 3 to 4.5 metres from the margins to its centre, and according to local inhabitants it appeared to be rising slowly. Aside from dwarfed blueberry bushes, the surface was "naked" of all growth. The bog itself was made of pure sphagnum, free from roots and showing no trace of decay or anything resembling muck. The living surface material merged downward into a matted, semi-peat-like material soaked in clear cold water. He confirmed its clarity by squeezing a handful of the moss, and its coldness by the speed with which it cooled "the liquid portion" of their lunch. On each side lay extensive flat bog of the ordinary kind that, in contrast to its raised neighbour, quaked when walked on.

Fully vindicated, his triumphant guide informed him of sixteen other bogs, varying in height from a metre up to about twelve or fifteen, along a narrow coastal strip in Charlotte and Saint John Counties. Obligated to provide an explanation for the Seely's Cove bog, Ganong suggested that the sphagnum through a sponge-like absorption of water from a large cold spring, or a line of small springs flowing from high land in the gravel beneath the bog, kept growing upward. As a hypothesis it was short-lived, the distinguished Danish botanist and plant ecologist Eugenius Warming demonstrating, in 1909, that sphagnum had little capacity to draw water upward by capillarity, and that to grow bogs needed no pre-existing water basin. In a sphagnum moor or bog the movement of water, Warming insisted, is essentially downward, and the level of the water table is determined by atmospheric precipitation and the permeability of the peat. Ganong attributed the absence of trees and shrubs on the Seely's Cove bog to the coldness of the water. Only cloudberry, a northern plant whose berries the locals gathered by the pail, could survive in it.

Ganong returned to bogs in the summers of 1895 and 1896, reporting his findings a year later in the *Transactions* of the Royal Society. Between Beaver Harbour in the west and Spruce Lake in the east he found twenty-four raised bogs within five miles of the coast, ranging in size from three to three hundred acres. All were a consequence of the frequent fogs, heavy rains, and cold waters of the Fundy coast, as well as the coolest summer temperatures in the province. Rates of evapotranspiration (a combination of physical evaporation and plant transpiration) were also low, accounting for a moisture surplus and perennial wetness. There were other bogs in the east and north at Caraquet, Miscou, and Richibuctou; none was as distinctly domed as the southern bogs, but they were more extensive and just as deep. His detailed examination of the largest bogs confirmed his earlier findings that the bogs were formed of pure sphagnum, growing upward and seeming to carry the water by capillarity with it. Impervious glacial clay deposits lay underneath them all.

Although holding to his capillarity hypothesis, Ganong was, as fellow botanist George Nichols indicated, puzzled by the immense amount of water held in their upper parts, some of which was three to four metres above general water levels, and by what prevented the water from flowing out under its own weight. Capillary action and the retentive strength of the interwoven sphagnum might not have been enough, and sometimes, as Ganong acknowledged, they were not. In Ireland and other parts of Europe, bogs unable to contain the accumulated weight of water had been known to burst with great damage to property and, in some cases, life. Ganong found no record of bog-bursts in North America.

In Europe, sphagnum moss's absorptive and antiseptic properties had prompted two contrasting uses. Sphagnum moss can absorb liquids up to twenty times its dry weight, making it an ideal substitute for absorbent cotton as a medical dressing, and a prized alternative to straw for bedding horses. New York stables imported it from Germany. Nitrogenous, it also made a good fertilizer when mixed with manure, and as a soil additive it increased the organic content and improved the soil's water-holding capacity. In New Brunswick the moss was available in almost unlimited quantities, but efforts to dry and market it failed. Labour costs were higher than in Germany, and the Fundy fogs and persistently high humidity delayed drying. At Spruce Lake in the early 1890s W. F. Todd, a St. Stephen entrepreneur, used a steam-driven machine to dig the moss from the bog and steam heat to dry it. He passed the moss through hot air chambers and pressed it into bales. The process took three hours, compared to three weeks by non-mechanical methods in Germany, and the finely divided product was said to have been superior. In 1915, however, the plant burned and was not rebuilt. On learning of Ganong's much earlier paper for the *Transactions*, Alfred Dachnowski of the Bureau of Plant Industry in the U.S. Department of Agriculture, whom Todd had consulted after the publication of Ganong's paper, in November 1924 wrote to Ganong to express his delight that his sounding of the Musquash bog and the ensuing "profile study" had corroborated Ganong's findings. He was also pleased to confirm Ganong's view that the bog had been formed in the post-Champlain period.

GRANDE PLAINE, MISCOU ISLAND

Ganong's third entry under the heading of "Contributions to the Plant Geography of New Brunswick" for the *Botanical Gazette*, was "The Nascent Forest of the Miscou Beach Plain." It appeared in 1906. Miscou is the last in a chain of islands and peninsulas angling out to sea in the far northeast of New Brunswick. On its western side is an extensive sandy beach plain, about a kilometre across at its widest, known locally as Grande Plaine. On it was a developing plant cover exhibiting every stage of formation from diminutive salt plants on the sea beach to a mixed-wood forest farther inland. Ganong spent three days on the island in 1904, and three weeks in August 1905, studying the physical geography, taking field notes, and collecting plants. His intention had been to write a report on the physical geography of the island, but Grande Plaine was of such ecological interest that he decided to write a separate report on it. Both reports appeared in 1906, that on the physical geography in the *Bulletin* of NHSNB. To be sure of his botanical identifications, Ganong sent a specimen of each plant collected to M. L. Fernald of the Gray Herbarium at Harvard who had, as Fernald put it, "poked about the Baie des Chaleurs coast somewhat." Fernald's interest was in the geographic origins and affinities of plants, and in his reply he noted that the collection contained certain plants, known to be common in Gaspé but reported by Ganong for the first time in New Brunswick. At Ganong's invitation Fernald retained fragments of eleven plants that were of particular interest to the Herbarium.

As an exercise in plant adaptation and succession in a rapidly changing beach environment, Ganong acknowledged his debt to Henry Chandler Cowles. On the southern shore of Lake Michigan, Cowles had shown that the natural succession of plant forms in time could be traced in physical space as one moved inland from the open lake beach through shifting dunes to the interior forest. Plants come into a landscape, flourish, and create conditions for their replacement by other plant communities. On Lake Michigan, scrubby beach grass gave way to flowers and woody plants inland: cottonwoods and pines yielded to oaks and hickories, and these to the climax forest of beeches and maples. The plant life of any community, he concluded, could be understood only as the product of constant flux and change within communities and between communities and their environs.

Cowles's background was in geology as well as botany, and he understood the close relationship between plant communities and the ground beneath. He called his field of research "physiographic plant ecology." So close was the relationship that he suggested there must be an order of succession in plant communities just as there is an order of succession of topographic forms in a landscape; as the years—or eons—pass, one plant society must necessarily be supplanted by another.

Ganong identified a succession similar to that on the shore of Lake Michigan in, as he described it, the plastic and unstable environment of Grande Plaine. Physiographically, Grande Plaine is an undulating plain, made up of a series of low concentric dune beaches, a metre to a metre and a half high, built by wind and waves on the northwest side of the island. At the narrow northern end of the beach, strong currents attacked the dunes and moved the sands and gravels south where, mixed with driftwood and weeds, they were washed ashore to form rough, longitudinal windrows. Windblown sand accumulated on these, and the result was a long, low dune. By 1905, about thirty of these dunes had coalesced in the middle of the plain to create an undulating surface of crests and hollows that, although vegetated for the most part, resembled, as Ganong described it, a frozen, gently swelling sea. Near the shore, the plain was open and treeless, clothed in gently waving beach grass. On the land side were woods that had obviously advanced from the upland, and between the grasses and the trees was a transition zone of close-tufted swales with park-like avenues and clumps of scattered trees.

Ganong described his work on Grande Plaine as entirely observational, performed without instruments or exact meteorological or soils data. He identified five vegetation zones: a beach zone of pure sand practically without vegetation; grass plains; swales; sandy woods; and close woods. Each dune began as a core of driftwood around which sand accumulated and on which, as the sand was driven inland, resilient deep-rooted beach grass gained a foothold and checked its further movement. The dry sand, however, moved inland faster than the beach grass could fix it, so the

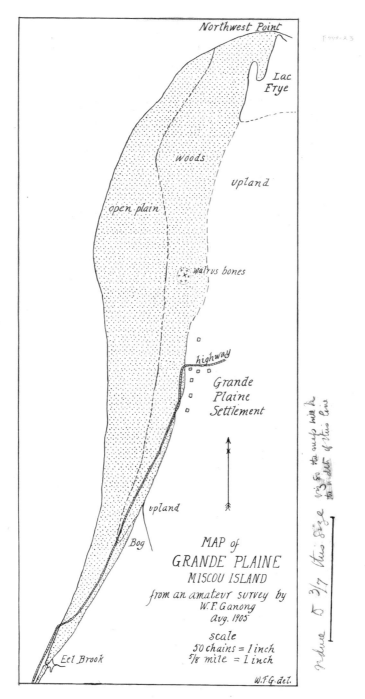

Northwest Point

Lac
Frye

Woods

upland

open plain

walrus bones

highway

Grande
Plaine
Settlement

upland

Bog

MAP of
GRANDE PLAINE
MISCOU ISLAND
from an amateur survey by
W. F. Ganong
aug. 1905

scale
50 chains = 1 inch
⅝ mile = 1 inch

Eel Brook

W. F. G. del.

reduce to ⅗ this size in so the map will be the width of this line

Ganong's map of the dune beach zone on the western shore of Miscou Island.

dunes could not grow to any considerable height. The beach grass made excellent hay and was cut and gathered by the Acadian inhabitants. It also provided, between its tussocks, shelter for a beach sedge, virtually the only other plant to seem, as Ganong put it, at home in the sand and wind. Sheltered from the westerly winds and nourished by a probable increase of mineral nutrients derived from decaying driftwood and some slight accumulation of humus, the leeward slopes were host to dense mats of creeping juniper, waxberry, and blueberry able to tolerate the dry, sandy conditions (physiological dryness). The juniper mats provided a woody net in which other dwarf forms could gain a foothold. These were the starting points that led gradually to forest.

In the more sheltered swales zone between the open grass plain and the woods was a transition zone of meadow turf and juniper mats in which small white spruce had rooted. Beyond these sometimes park-like areas were the sandy woods of older and larger white spruce and, beyond the sandy woods, dense though dwarfed mixed woods extending to the upland. The closed woods consisted essentially of more juniper mats, which united to form a complete unbroken carpet, together with a greater development, both in number and size, of the white spruce trees to which were added some deciduous trees and shrubs. These woods, excepting the size of plants, were not markedly different from the preponderantly coniferous woods in the neighbouring upland. Evidently tending toward the typical mixed coniferous-deciduous forest woods, they were demonstrating a principle of "physiognomic" ecology: that vegetation, no matter what the immediate physical conditions may be, is always tending toward a climax type, determined principally by climate.

In spite of his detailed accounting of the plants in each zone, Ganong realized that his study was more an exercise in plant geography than ecology—an attempt to relate broad patterns in the plant cover to various environmental factors. If asked why the white spruce was the first to develop on the plains as opposed to some other of the upland species, he would not have been able to answer. To advance ecology, what was needed were studies that monitored the effects of particular environmental conditions on individual plants or small groups of plants. Interpretive work, as distinct from the kind of descriptive work he could do, would depend

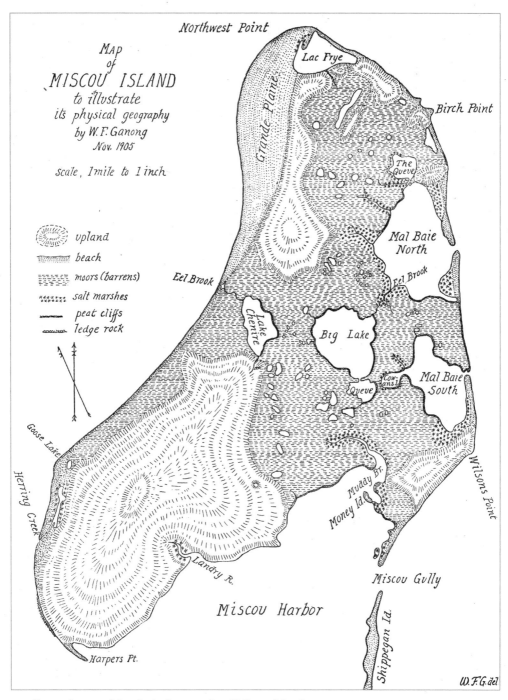

Map
of
MISCOU ISLAND
to illustrate
its physical geography
by W. F. Ganong
Nov. 1905

scale, 1 mile to 1 inch

upland
beach
moors (barrens)
salt marshes
peat cliffs
ledge rock

Northwest Point

Lac Frye

Birch Point

Grande Plaine

The Queue

Mal Baie North

Eel Brook

Eel Brook

Lake Chenire

Big Lake

Mal Baie South

Queue

Cowans Id.

Goose Lake

Herring Creek

Muddy Br.

Money Id.

Wilsons Point

Landry R.

Miscou Gully

Miscou Harbor

Shippegan Id.

Harpers Pt.

W.F.G. del

Ganong's map of the physical geography of Miscou Island. NEW BRUNSWICK MUSEUM,
GANONG COLLECTION: S224-F450-14-1

on field physiologists working out, in field laboratories, the fundamentals of plant dynamics. These, as Ganong saw it, fell under three heads: the physiological life histories of species, the physics and chemistry of the soil, and the nature of plant competition.

Ganong's textbooks, his work on cacti, and his much praised study of the Fundy marshes led to his appointment to the council of the Society for Plant Morphology and Physiology and for nine years as its corresponding secretary until it was absorbed by the Botanical Society of America. In 1908–09 he bettered this with the award of the (second) presidency of the Botanical Society of America. His Bay of Fundy and Miscou Plain studies, however, were as far as he would take ecological and botanical research. In his retirement address as president of the Botanical Society of America in 1909 he announced that he was, in effect, giving up both. There had been intimations earlier of the conflict between teaching and research and how, as implied in the Bay of Fundy study, the kind of detailed laboratory research on which advances depended could best be carried on by specialists in research institutions equipped with the kind of facilities that a small college could not afford. Research was fundamental to universities but only incidental to colleges, whose role was the organization and dissemination of existing knowledge rather than the discovery of new. Ganong's study of the Fundy marshlands and Grande Plaine had been entirely observational and not at all instrumental, and performed without the aid of any meteorological or other precise physical data. From now on, as a botanist, Ganong would concentrate on teaching. He admitted that it had taken many years to subdue the feeling that he must concentrate on research in order not to sacrifice the good opinion of his colleagues, but now he felt like Sinbad who had shaken from his shoulders the old man of the sea. He encouraged fellow college professors, who felt burdened by research, to follow his example. Ganong, of course, had no intention of giving up research and writing. Disinclined to engage in intensive laboratory work, he was simply heading in another direction—toward New Brunswick, his country.

Chapter 4

$\sim$

LIMNING A COUNTRY

At the end of the nineteenth century, parts of New Brunswick were still *terrae incognitae,* country that had been neither explored nor mapped. The broad outlines of the province's geography and history had been sketched, but there were few details and a great many blanks. In a 1986 interview the historian Alfred G. Bailey, son of Professor Loring Woart Bailey and an early curator of the New Brunswick Museum, remarked that in Ganong's day New Brunswick had little sense of itself as a province. Unlike Nova Scotia and Prince Edward Island, its shape was not memorable, and its name, unlike Nova Scotia's, conveyed no immediate meaning. Alone among the Canadian provinces, it had no archives and had no firm sense of its own development. The strongest feelings, as suggested by the response of volunteers at the outbreak of the First World War seem to have been for the empire and the crown ("for Jarge," as new recruits used to say) rather than the region or the province.

Community and provincial records had been so neglected that when the Department of Agriculture asked Ganong if he would give them a copy of his monograph on the origins of settlements he agreed on condition that it be chained to a desk. When looking in the legislative library and government departments for information on immigration to the province, he had been unable to find a single collection of official reports and papers. Ganong set out to correct this. He was told that there would be legislative records in the attic of the old Government House in Fredericton that had been closed since 1890 and was used for storage. When he got there some of the documents had been burned and dumped in the river. According to Bailey, Ganong hired a buggy and loaded up the rest. That, said Bailey, was the beginning of the Ganong Collection.

What Ganong had in mind was a comprehensive physical and historical geography that would be a founding block for a society of, as he phrased it, the highest quality. Ganong's strengths were close studies of land and people, somewhat in the manner of French historians and geographers, although these would not have been his models. Political, constitutional, and economic history were not prime interests, and in any case he thought they were beyond his range, requiring a facility with language and flights of imagination he felt he did not possess, and in effect feared. "A history of mine would be coldly scientific, precise, classified, complete; but it would lack the life and form and colour which should distinguish a history for the people." As an historian he described himself as a pre-Raphaelite: a precise, small-details man, a pointillist not a brush-waving Romantic. He was content to labour in what he regarded as the foothills, authenticating and recording sites, dates, and names before these were lost. He visited places, interviewed the residents, gathered documentary and cartographic evidence and, when necessary, excavated ruins to establish accuracy. Interpretation and synthesis, the higher reaches of history as he described them, he left to minds he considered more adventurous and voluminous than his own. His contributions, as he put it, with touching but exaggerated self-effacement, were to history much as dictionaries were to literature.

At Harvard and Smith College—and even at Munich—New Brunswick was never far from Ganong's mind; despite the demands of teaching and research he continued to write about it. As he settled into his career as a professor of botany, he devoted more and more time to New Brunswick. Teaching botany and running a six- to seven-member department offering a full range of courses in botany and horticulture was his winter job; summers and, presumably, many winter evenings were taken up by New Brunswick. Ganong's second wife, Anna Hobbet—whom he had married in 1923—described him retiring to his study/library and map room every evening and not re-emerging until bedtime. Yet he was also thoroughly involved in life at Smith. He loved teaching, and as the college's provost marshal he organized many of the college rituals and ceremonies. Only after commencement exercises in late June was he free to leave Northampton for New Brunswick, returning in late August or early September for the next academic year. To his friend and fellow ethnographer Fannie Eckstorm, he confided moving between scientific and historical research kept him alert and interested in both.

The vehicles for his New Brunswick history were five book-length monographs, published under the heading of "Contributions to the History of New Brunswick," in the *Transactions of the Royal Society of Canada* (TRSC). They first appeared in 1895, the year following his return from Munich, and the last in 1906. In effect, they were a series of detailed lessons for provincial readers that, collectively, amounted to a comprehensive history or historical geography. Combined, they ran to more than a thousand printed pages. His subjects ran the gamut from the mapping and naming of the province, the evolution of its boundaries, its physical geography, its historic sites and settlements, and the origins and distribution of its ordinary, everyday ones. In a letter to G. R. F. Prowse written in 1897, Ganong described them as preliminary in character, little more than roughly organized base materials for a projected comprehensive history that he would never finish. Yet without a book, as the astronomer Francois Arago told Alexander von Humboldt, a naturalist and polymath who operated on a much larger stage than Ganong, his writings would be a portrait without a frame. In 1895 Ganong produced an outline for the Royal Society that began with the physiography and natural history of the province and worked its way through exploration, settlement, and economic history until Confederation. Later, he wrote chapters on physiography, topography, and cartography, but these remain in manuscript form in the archives of the New Brunswick Museum.

CARTOGRAPHY

For readers of the series in *Transactions*, an early lesson was to demonstrate how a nondescript part of the planet acquired, in Shakespeare's phrase, "a local habitation and a name." How, from "airy nothing" the poet's (cartographer's) pen had fashioned a place from previously undifferentiated space. Until mapped and named, a place has no fixed existence, no place in our consciousness. Ganong described the process: "It is a matter of extreme interest to follow the gradual crystallizing...of a given region from the great...undifferentiated mass of which at first it is an unrecognizable part, and to trace...the gradual unfolding of its outlines and the definition of its boundaries."

He began his systematic study of the cartography in 1887 with an account, in the TRSC, of Jacques Cartier's 1534 voyage along the north shore of the province. His friend and fellow historian of cartography, G. R. F. Prowse, would describe it as astonishing for its balance and maturity. Ganong was twenty-three at the time. In 1889 he extended his geographical range with a second article for *Transactions* on the early mapping of the Gulf of St. Lawrence. To avoid upsetting established historians of cartography, he opened with a disclaimer, reassuring them that he viewed the subject from the standpoint of local history, not scientific cartography. "I have been interested less in what New Brunswick maps illustrate of the principles of cartography, than what they teach about New Brunswick history." Throughout his career he chose the concrete and the particular over the abstract and the generalized.

Despite his disclaimer, Ganong quickly came to be regarded as the authority on the province's historical maps. In 1897–98, three years after completing his Ph.D. and about a year before the publication of *The Teaching Botanist*, he wrote a 120-page monograph on the mapping of the province for the *Transactions*. The process of giving shape and form to previously undifferentiated space might have enthralled him, but his treatment of it was coolly scientific. He saw in maps, as in the forms of nature, evidence of Darwinian selection: only the fittest maps, or the fittest parts of them, survived to be passed on to the next generation. He considered classifying maps into families, genera and species, but not all could be accommodated, so he settled for a classification into types, named after groundbreaking explorers and cartographers. Far from forming a steadily improving graded sequence, as one might suppose, the general maps of the province fall into a series of steps based upon the epoch-making work of some leading explorer or cartographer. Between each epoch-making work were long intervals marked by repetition without improvement, and even reversion and error.

The first known explorer in eastern Canada was the Venetian Giovanni Caboto (John Cabot) who arrived in 1497 under the patronage of Henry VII of England. Cabot's own narratives and maps were lost, but maps based on information he provided suggest that he merely skirted the north shore of what is now New Brunswick. On the fabricated map, it appears as a crinkled and unbroken coastline. Like all early explorers, Cabot used a compass for general directions and a log and dead reckoning (a crude method based on estimated rates of sailing) for estimating distances.

Mapping the Atlantic coast began with Jacques Cartier in 1534; the king of France had instructed him to explore the new land, assess its resources, and look for a western passage to Cathay. Cartier's original maps were also lost, but his narratives and contemporary compilations allowed a reconstruction of his voyages and his cartography. He came into the Gulf of St. Lawrence through the Straits of Belle Isle, and after touching the north coast of PEI he entered the head of Northumberland Strait. He mistook this for an enclosed bay, and after turning around he sailed into the mouth of the Miramichi River, describing it as "a triangular bay [ringed] with sands." Coasting northward, Cartier rounded Cap Miscou, which he named Cap d'Espérance (*espérance* is French for hope, a name which Ganong wished be retained) hoping it might lead to Cathay. He entered the warmer waters of the Baie des Chaleurs, which name did survive (as Chaleur Bay), and sailed to the head of the bay along the north coast.

Ganong hailed Cartier's successor, Samuel de Champlain, as a model explorer and recorder: Champlain had sailed down the St. Lawrence in 1603 and elicited details of the North Shore and Prince Edward Island from the Aboriginals of Gaspé. He separated PEI from the mainland, which Cartier had not done, and except for Chaleur Bay, abandoned the earlier naming. He was a trained map-maker and dealt, Ganong remarked admiringly, in new truths, mapping only what he had seen or learned of directly from good authority. Ganong considered his *Voyages de la Nouvelle France* to be a great book of exploration, the equal of Xenophon's *Anabasis*. In the preface to his 1929 translation (with H. H. Langton, Librarian of the University of Toronto), of the first volume of the *Voyages* for the Champlain Society, Ganong noted he had covered most of the ground mapped or described by Champlain. In the case of his special maps, he did so with a minuteness that astonished the critic for the *Toronto Globe*: "His [Ganong's] explanatory notes and critical comments are beyond praise: one cannot recall anything of this kind quite so complete and so illuminating in the whole range of North American historical study. It is seldom that a historian examines an engraving or a drawing with a critical faculty equal to that which he brings to bear upon a written or a printed document, but Professor Ganong reads a map or a picture with the same sympathetic understanding as he does a text."

Ganong reported that instead of loosely written narratives and maps that bore very little relation to the places they described, Champlain's descriptions of the coasts he visited were remarkably accurate. As a fellow map-maker, Ganong understood the difficulties of representing topography on a flat sheet of paper. With only a compass for measuring angles and dead reckoning for gauging distances, Champlain was restricted to one vantage point. Later map-makers could make measurements and calculate distances by taking angles from fixed places. Early map-makers also had to contend with wind, weather, weariness, and, in Ganong's phrase, "the exceeding speed of time." In spite of the obstacles, Ganong regarded Champlain's maps as prototypes of our own, inferior in technique but their equal in conception. Ganong asserted that Champlain initiated the modern—"one can almost say scientific"—cartography of New Brunswick.

Champlain began his exploration of the Bay of Fundy, which he mapped on a large scale, in 1604. He coasted around the Nova Scotia peninsula and explored the bay as far north as Cape Chignecto before crossing to the New Brunswick shore. From there he sailed west to the St. John and the St. Croix Rivers, naming the St. John after the saint on whose day (June 24) he arrived there. A red sandstone cape at the entrance to the river he named Cap de Rouge, now Red Head. He and his party wintered on an island a few miles above the mouth of the St. Croix, and the following spring they established a permanent settlement across the Bay of Fundy at Port Royal. Working from hasty traverses (longitudinal lines of sight), Champlain's other major cartographic achievement was to map the entire Canadian and New England coast from Cape Sable to Cape Cod.

Mapping of the interior began in the seventeenth century with Jesuit and Recollet missionaries who made maps and sketches of the country they crossed and sent them to France. By the middle of the eighteenth century the large rivers, main avenues for travel, had been sketched, but in the absence of topographical surveys there were no detailed, large-scale maps. Coastal areas, however, fared better. To administer territories won during the Seven Years' War (1756–1763), England required accurate maps and charts. The Board of Admiralty commissioned trained cartographers Charles Morris, Thomas Wright, and Frederick DesBarres to conduct coast and harbour surveys. These and the topographic sketches that accompanied them were later collected into the four-volume atlas called *The Atlantic Neptune*. The historian E. E. Rich described it as the most splendid collection of charts, views, and plans ever published. The charts were beautifully engraved with the land areas, to indicate vertical topography, ornamented by a combination of hachures (fine radiating lines to indicate the direction and speed at which water would run down a slope) and tone shading. In addition to the charts there were views, engraved in copperplate and hand-coloured, of the entrance to the St. John River, Campobello, and the mainland. "Through them all," Ganong wrote judiciously, "runs the beauty of copper-plate engraving and hand colouring, though the conventional land topography is not to be trusted in detail."

Other notable cartographic achievements of the period, cited by Ganong, were the French engineer L'Hermitte's 1724 chart of the coast from Miramichi to Restigouche, so accurate it could only have been based on near-modern survey methods, and Charles Morris's map of Chignecto Bay. Then an officer in the British navy and a leading cartographer, Morris became Surveyor General for Nova Scotia. To illustrate

General Monckton's journal of his 1758 expedition, Morris mapped the lower St. John on a relatively large scale indicating its French settlements, the only cartographer to do so. After separation from Nova Scotia in 1784, New Brunswick had a Crown Land and a Surveyor General's office and surveyors of its own. Independence prompted further exploration, especially of accessible areas that might be suitable for settlement.

By 1820, the shaping or definition of the province was almost complete. Earlier maps had shown the province only as part of North America, New France, or Nova Scotia. But in 1820 New Brunswick had a map all to itself. Its author, but probably not the draughtsman, was Thomas Bonnor, the Provincial Agent in London from 1816–1824. Published in London at a scale of eight miles to the inch, Bonnor's map was the sum, as Ganong put it, of then existing knowledge. Old errors were corrected and unexplored areas were left blank. On the main route to Quebec, the upper courses of the St. John, the St. Croix, and the Restigouche Rivers were shown in some detail, but only the lower courses of the Tobique and the Nepisiguit received equivalent treatment. The course of the Miramichi was precise as far upstream as Boiestown but shown only sketchily above. The upper courses of small streams were simply approximated with broken lines. Counties were named, but no boundaries were assigned to them.

As well as adding detail, later cartographers embellished their maps. In 1832 Thomas Baillie, surveyor general for New Brunswick, and Lieutenant Edward Kendall produced a copperplate map, "beautifully executed," according to Ganong, at a scale of ten miles to the inch. Most of the streams were drawn accurately, and the granted lands were all marked.

Even more accurate, and just as finely worked, was John Wilkinson's 1859 provincial map. A graduate of the Institute of Civil Engineers in London, Wilkinson came to the country in 1830 to manage the Owen estate at Campobello. He died in Fredericton in 1871. Of all the surveyors and cartographers to work in the province, he was the most highly trained. He surveyed county lines, early railway routes, and the international boundary, and after several years of uninterrupted work he published his 1859 official map of New Brunswick. It was the first general map to incorporate admiralty surveys, boundary surveys, and accumulated

Crown Land surveys. Ganong described it as "scientifically constructed, minutely correct," and "beautifully engraved." He pronounced, "It must ever remain a classic of New Brunswick cartography."

Although distances were fairly accurate on early maps, few indicated height or relief. In some, hachuring was used to represent hills, but none had contour lines. Even the best maps had large gaps where there was no indication of topography or where broken lines approximated upper stream courses. No lumberman or outdoorsman, Ganong noted, needed to be told how inaccurately mapped were the streams and lakes in wilderness areas; Ganong devoutly and frequently wished for a trigonometrical survey of the entire province. Maps of small areas might be true, but maps of large areas could be made only by piecing together surveys of different ages, scales, and authority. Accuracy was a pipe dream. The only published maps using contour lines were a crude folder, issued by a steamboat company, showing hills beside the St. John River and a coastal strip between Waweig and St. Stephen mapped by the United States Coast Survey. The latter was the most accurately mapped part of the province. Capt. W. F. W. Owen surveyed the lower Saint John Valley from its mouth to Springhill in the early 1840s, but his fine contour maps were never published.

To underline the need for a provincial topographic survey, Ganong listed the advantages of contour maps. Among the first to appreciate them were soldiers. Maps that showed topography and revealed lines of sight at a glance were invaluable to marksmen and artillery. Cadets at Woolwich, the training school for British officers, were expected to "draw ground," or provide topographic sketches that revealed the lay of the land. Civilian uses for accurate topographic maps were legion, from the planning of routes for roads and railways and assessments of water power potential to determining both private and official boundaries. Ganong's unrealizable ideal was province-wide coverage at a horizontal scale of one half mile to the inch and a contour interval of twenty feet. For an admirable model of modern map-making he referred readers to Henry Gannett's *Topographic Atlas of the United States*. Maine-born Gannett was Chief Geographer for the U.S. Geological Survey and a founding member of both the National Geographic Society and the American Association of Geographers. In 1893, he wrote *A Manual of Topographic Methods*, the first book to establish rules for the conduct of topographic surveys. In several ways Gannett was Ganong's precursor (he was a generation older), writing continually for journals, scientific magazines, and encyclopedias on subjects that ranged from mapping and boundaries, to river systems, the origin of place names, economic geography, and statistical population studies. In response to a letter from Ganong, Gannett suggested that a horizontal scale of two miles to the inch, the scale adopted by the United States, should serve New Brunswick's needs.

At the top of Ganong's want list for the province, published by *Acadiensis* in 1904, was a topographical survey at one mile to the inch, larger than Gannett's suggested scale. Ganong was musing on what gifts he would bestow on the province should he inherit a large fortune.

All the details of this survey I have thought out, even to such par-
ticulars as the wording of the letter in which I ask the Legislature to
accept it on behalf of the province....First to come is the Geographical
or Topographical division, whose duty it is, with proper triangulations
and other exact methods, to furnish a minutely accurate map of the prov-
ince on a scale of a mile to an inch, with much enlarged maps of import-
ant localities near the cities. These maps are of course to show contours,
with all important heights determined by spirit level, and every other
topographical feature. Great numbers of large photographs will further
illustrate the topography, and the scenery as well; and I have worked out
a very ingenious system for correlating the photographs with the maps, so
that the observer may be able exactly to fit the one to the other.

EVOLUTION OF THE BOUNDARIES

The longest of the monographs in the New Brunswick series, and the most widely read and acclaimed because it touched on the histories of Maine and neighbouring provinces, was the 312-page "Evolution of the Boundaries" (1901). Ganong justified its length on grounds that it was the first study of all the province's boundaries and that no comprehensive history or geography could proceed without some understanding of the procedures by which the province had been framed. These were so complex, he ventured, that in no other country or state of similar size could boundary disputes have been more aggravating: "so often and so conspicuously in contention, so fully discussed by many and weighty commissions, and so inseparable from its general history." Not that he thought Americans and Britons were particularly intransigent, but disputes over land and territory exposed our worst sides not our best. Given our territoriality, our quick defence of caste or clan, and our tendency to reject all views incompatible with our own self-interests, there are few issues over which, in his succinct phrase, "nations were more ready to go war, or individuals to law." Better, he thought, to remove immediately ambiguities over boundaries and, with them, any remaining resentments over perceived injustices.

Ganong began the book-length TRSC monograph with an assessment of the physical features commonly chosen to define external boundaries. The most effective are those that naturally separate people: seas and lakes and prominent hill and mountain ranges. The least effective, although frequently chosen, are rivers. Rivers are visible, they require no survey, and except in soft, easily eroded flood plains, they don't move. The drawback is that they unite rather than divide communities. Most rivers, unless wild or very wide, are easily crossed by boat or bridge and people living on opposing banks are more likely than not to be of a common culture or community, "people of the valley." Watersheds that divide river basins are far more effective, and the higher they are the better. In New Brunswick, the Maliseet and the Mi'kmaq regarded the watersheds as band or tribal boundaries, and the Loyalists who followed used them to define administrative units.

Sea on the eastern and southern sides of the province, and a narrow isthmus connecting it to Nova Scotia, removed occasions for dispute of the external boundaries. Inland, however, and in the island-studded waters of the southwest, boundary disputes were fraught and often interminable. The most contentious, and at times abrasive, of them was over the international boundary with Maine and the United States. At the Paris Peace Conference, 1783, the British and American commissioners agreed on the St. Croix or the Schoodic as the divide between the United States and British North America. This begged the question, however, of which of the rivers flowing into Passamaquoddy Bay was the true St. Croix, the river up which Champlain had sailed and named and where he and his party attempted to settle. Americans opted for the most easterly river, the Magaguadavic, and the British for the most westerly, the Schoodic. The matter was not finally resolved until 1797 when Robert Pagan of St. Andrews discovered five distinct piles of worked stone foundations (a clear indication of the intent to settle) at the site of the French settlement on diminutive Dochet's Island, near the mouth of the Schoodic. The Schoodic, therefore, was Champlain's St. Croix. Dochet's, or St. Croix, Island is one of the smallest islands ever to figure in a great international dispute.

In the 1880s the identity of the St. Croix may no longer have been seriously in question, but sometime before 1887 Justin Winsor, librarian at Harvard and an eminent historian of early colonization and cartography, visited St. Croix Island to check the physical evidence of the Champlain settlement. Winsor found nothing conclusive on the island but was told that field stones from the original settlement may have been worked into the foundation of a cottage that carried on its roof a United States coast lantern. The island is on the American side of the border.

Although volumes had already been written on the question of the identity of the St. Croix, to dispel any gnawing American resentments Ganong felt it necessary to respond to the question raised by Winsor's visit. For an 1891 article in the *Magazine of American History*, he surveyed the early cartography, and drawing on his extensive knowledge of Aboriginal place names he was able to identify a lake at the head of the river shown on Mitchell's 1763 map as the source of the St. Croix, strengthening the argument that the commissioners had chosen the right river. He concluded the choice of the St. Croix as the boundary river had been "a happy one, and one which should remove the cause, even though a slight one, of irritation between two peoples who should be bound together by the closest ties of social and political friendship."

Also in dispute at the time of the peace was the primacy of the two branches or tributaries that joined to form the St. Croix. The British agent claimed that the headwaters of the western branch were the true source, whereas the American agent made the same claim for the eastern branch, the Chiputneticook. After much debate, the commissioners settled on the eastern branch, the boundary running from Joe's Point near St. Andrews to a monument at the head of the Chiputneticook. From there the line was to run due north to the "highlands," the watershed that separates the rivers flowing into the St. Lawrence from those flowing into the Atlantic.

In the south, however, the boundary question did not end at Joe's Point. Between the mouth of the St. Croix and the open waters of the Bay of Fundy is a jigsaw of islands that the boundary commissioners had to thread their way through. The only island beyond dispute was

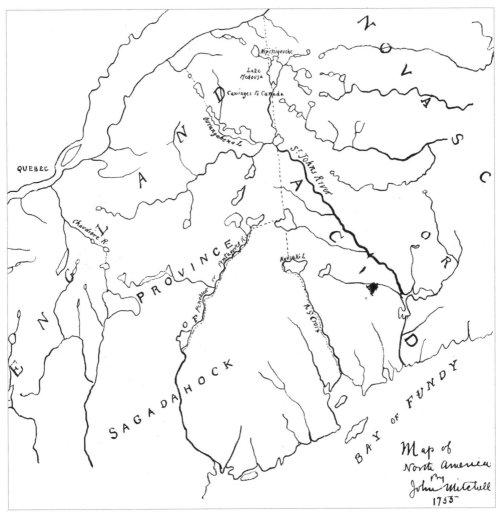

Ganong's copy of part of John Mitchell's 1775 map of the Bay of Fundy. New Brunswick Museum, Ganong Collection: F449-15

Moose Island (Eastport) without which the United States would have no access to the St. Croix and the inner bay of Passamaquoddy, other than by special arrangement with Great Britain. The Commission assembled at Boston in 1817, and the British and American agents presented their memorials. These, together with the journals of the Commission, amounted to eight folio volumes. The British agent's memorial was a document of 135 pages, the American's 459 pages. The intent, Ganong concluded, was to create an impression of bigness and importance rather than to present arguments that had any expectation of being read carefully. Many of the documents he dismissed as "appallingly and uselessly diffuse." The final settlement, he conceded, was extremely favourable to New Brunswick. The United States was granted Moose Island, and with it undisputed passage to the inner bay of Passamaquoddy, but New Brunswick got everything else. Ganong pointed out that if the boundary had been drawn on strictly natural or practical geographic grounds, then Campobello, separated from Maine by a narrow channel, and Grand Manan, closer to Maine than New Brunswick and settled by New Englanders, would have been ceded to the U.S.

The northwest boundary with Maine was not settled until the sign- ing of the Webster-Ashburton Treaty in 1842. By the terms of the 1784 treaty, the line was to run due north from the source of the St. Croix to the "highlands" or watershed dividing the St. Lawrence and Atlantic drain- age systems. The country was not settled and the exact line never deter- mined. Only after the St. Andrews–Quebec railway company announced its intention to run a line through the unassigned territory in 1836 was there need for an official agreement. The boundary finally accepted by both parties was a line running north from the source of the St. Croix to the St. John at Grand Falls and then following the river. It was the route advocated in the 1784 treaty and later endorsed by the King of Holland, the arbitrator of a dispute in the 1820s.

Although many New Brunswickers were aggrieved by the final settle- ment, Ganong argued that the province at no time had legal claim to lands west of the north–south line. The misfortune of the agreement was the division of the Acadian settlement at Madawaska by the choice of the river boundary. Alexander Baring (Lord Ashburton), the British commissioner, refused to yield on Great Britain's possession of the

Temiscouata river route (the main route to Quebec), and Maine would give up territory north of there only if compensated. Grand Manan and Campobello were the suggested bargaining chips, but Maine had to settle for free navigation on the lower St. John for agricultural and forest products. Although legally correct, Ganong described Maine's behaviour in

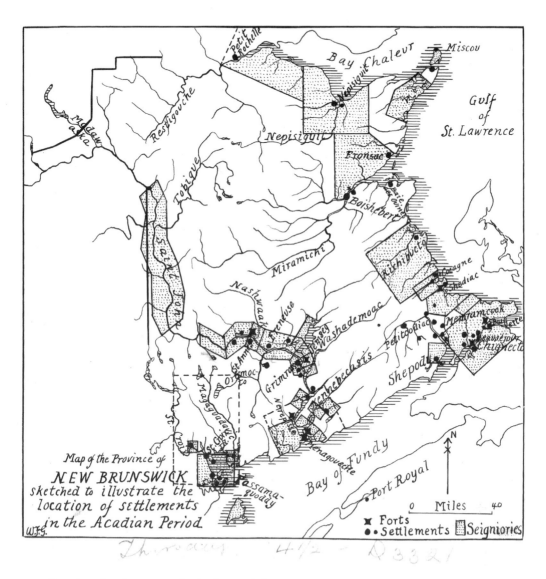

Location of settlements in the Acadian period. NEW BRUNSWICK MUSEUM, GANONG COLLECTION: F448-10

demanding territory north of the St. John, which the people of Maine had neither explored nor settled, as "Shylockian." Maine had not placed a single settler upon it nor built a road to it for half a century after the treaty was signed, whereas the territory had been settled in good faith by British subjects and was indispensable to Great Britain as a link between New Brunswick and the Canadas. Ganong's use of the term *Shylockian* offended Henry S. Burrage, the Maine State Librarian and an eminent historian, who delivered a stiff rejoinder in a subsequent book on the northeastern boundary controversy. Burrage, however, admired Ganong's work, and the two eventually made up. In a typescript elsewhere, Ganong noted that a positive effect of the boundary controversies, from which both nations benefited, was the incentive given to the exploration and mapping of the upper St. John, Green River, and Madawaska regions, and large parts of the interior of Maine.

Although many New Brunswickers were disgruntled about having to give up territory south of the St. John, Ganong was adamant about the legality of the settlement. By not insisting on Mars Hill or a more southerly latitude for the boundary, earlier commissioners, not Lord Ashburton, were to be blamed for allowing a wedge of Maine to be pushed upward into New Brunswick. Ganong conceded, however, that in 1783 any proposition to the American commissioners that part of Massachusetts be ceded to Nova Scotia in order to facilitate communications to Canada would have been met with "fine scorn." The effect of the wedge was to prevent direct access to Quebec and to increase, both actually and perceptually, the distance between the Maritimes and the rest of Canada. Although the CPR would run a line through northern Maine, the St. Andrews–Quebec railway was forced to make a long detour.

The resolution of New Brunswick–Quebec boundary, which ought to have been straightforward, was also convoluted. Ganong's monograph on boundaries contained the first ever analysis of the issues. The western boundary, legally established in 1784, was to be the line running due north from the source of the St. Croix to the highlands separating the St. Lawrence and Atlantic drainage systems. Trouble began when the surveyor general for Quebec, in 1785, questioned whether Lake Temiscouata and the drainage from it (the Madawaska River), south of the height of land, ought not to belong to Quebec. A line run due north from the source of the St. Croix would run east of the Madawaska River and Lake Temiscouata, leaving them outside Quebec. By the same measure, Quebec had no authority south of the northern highland. Madawaska was in limbo, neither province able to claim ownership, although New Brunswick never relinquished its claim to lands west of the north–south line to which, as Ganong pointed out, the Americans might have made

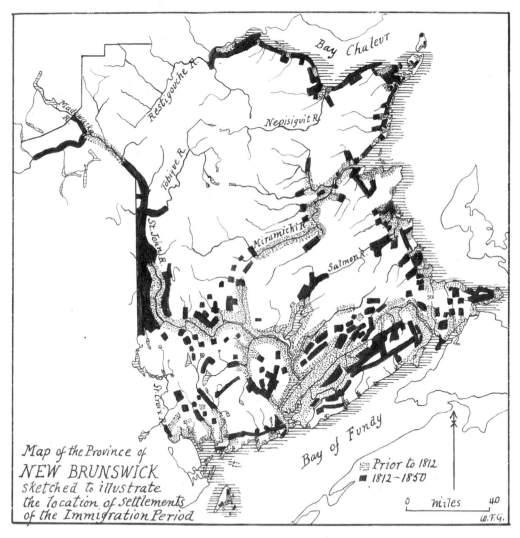

Location of settlements in the immigration period in New Brunswick, 1812–1850.

a stronger claim. The respective surveyors general met in 1787 but could not reach an agreement, and there the matter stood for decades. In the meantime, New Brunswick in 1787 granted licences of occupation along the Madawaska to Acadians unsettled by the advance of Loyalists up the Saint John valley above Fredericton. The Acadians wished to remain under a New Brunswick government. Settlement would be a badge of ownership, and settlers would help maintain the vital military and postal route to Quebec. As the only river route, it was crucial not to let the lands fall into American hands.

After the signing of the Webster/Ashburton Treaty in 1842, questions about the ownership of land and timber between Quebec and New Brunswick surfaced again. To strengthen its claims, New Brunswick exercised jurisdiction through land surveys in the disputed territory, and in 1845 Governor Colebrooke conceded that whatever the legal rights in the matter, the boundary issue had resolved itself into a question of possession. To break the deadlock, in 1846 Westminster intervened. Home Secretary Gladstone, overwhelmed by the amount of documentation, commissioned two engineer officers and a lawyer to explore the region and, in effect, cut through the documentation. Their report, coming down on the side of possession and jurisdiction, was decisive. "The inhabitants of this portion of the country have chiefly settled under the authority of New Brunswick, and are familiar with the administration of its laws and usages; and the St. John and its tributaries, the Madawaska and the St. Francis, offer to them, through New Brunswick, the most eligible mode of transport to market for their timber and other products of the country." Arbitration followed, modifying but largely accepting the conclusion of the 1848 commission.

In his long monograph for the TRSC, which included the first ever analysis of the New Brunswick–Quebec border issue, Ganong concluded New Brunswick might have lost some ground to Maine south of the northern watershed, but the province had gained far more than it was entitled to west of the north–south line and that even the minor points of the settlement were in New Brunswick's favour. In this and the other border settlements, he insisted, New Brunswick had done rather well, and there was no cause for resentment.

NAMING AND TOPONOMY

For Europeans naming, like mapping, was a form of possession, and in practice they worked together, defining the geography and serving as, in Ganong's phrase, "marvellously persistent memorials of past events and conditions," charting the history. Elsewhere in the monograph he described them as a permanent register or index, "fossils exposed in the cross-section of...history, marking its successive periods." In his book *Place Names of Atlantic Canada* (1996), W. B. Hamilton declared Ganong's 1896 study remained "a standard reference, not only for the place names of his native province, but also in the principles of research in place nomenclature."

The most common place names are descriptive. In New Brunswick, the earliest (and still among the most numerous) were Aboriginal. Europeans adopted them freely, particularly the French who were allies of the First Nations. Most describe natural features: rivers, lakes, and harbours in particular, underlining the crucial importance of waterways for travel in heavily wooded country and the critical importance of landmarks to nomadic, hunting and gathering peoples. Because they had meaning and were not simply labels, they were clues or keys to the topography. Applied to particular places or particular features such as rocks, bends, or rapids, and noting the idiosyncrasies of each, they were also specific. A river might be tidal (flowing both ways), swift, slow flowing, or a place where eels might be caught and animals congregate. It was never just a river.

On the other hand, Aboriginals had no names for large stretches of country, suggesting they had little or no concept of landscape. The association of Miramichi, Restigouche, and Westmorland with particular kinds of terrain is strictly European. Fannie Hardy Eckstorm, the American (Maine) ethnologist and folklorist, pointed out that without maps—and surrounded always by tall trees—without vistas, the Aboriginals might never have had a bird's-eye view of country. She advised Ganong that, in order to see the world through Aboriginal eyes, the European gaze should never rise above ground or water level. The Aboriginals' viewpoint was that of a canoeist. "I have tried to make myself an Indian far back before white folks came," she wrote, "and tried to see what he saw.

It was all big pine here then and the growth covered everything. Except from Thomas's Hill in Bangor…there was no place in miles about from which you could get any extended view."

As explorers, the navigators named only prominent or striking features in the landscape. In 1534, Jacques Cartier on the North Shore named the promontory at the mouth of the Restigouche on the north shore "Cap d'Espérance," hoping it pointed the way to Cathay; the name was later changed to "Point Miscou." The warm waters lapping its shores he called "Baie des Chaleurs." Champlain, who was the last of the official explorers, left a handful of names in the Bay of Fundy in 1604, but he seldom used Aboriginal names.

After Champlain, the naming of the province passed to missionary priests and traders. The close relationship between the French and the Mi'kmaq and Maliseet led naturally to the near-automatic adoption of names of Native origin, and by the same token strained relations between the French and the English and the enforced removal of the former had the opposite effect. Wherever there was a choice, the English substituted English names for the French. Ganong cited General Monckton's 1758 map of the Saint John valley in which French names are more numerous than they were in Ganong's day. The Expulsion of the Acadians itself left no trace in place names, but it removed many that would now still exist. An ironic survivor of the episode is Burnt Church on the north shore; the name refers to a punitive English expedition against the French in 1758 that led to the burning of the timbers and the destruction of a stone church.

At the head of the Bay of Fundy Ganong pointed to several names to which a French origin of fanciful character is commonly given. Among them: Shepody, said to be a corruption of Chapeau Dieu (God's hat); Minudie, a corruption of Main-à-Dieu (God's hand); and Chignecto, a corruption of Chignon du Col (nape of the neck). The form and history of the words point unmistakably to an Aboriginal origin whereas others, such as Tantramar and Aulac, are truly French in form and origin. In the case of landforms, on the other hand, Acadian names might have supplanted the English. Ganong cited gully, from *goulet*, the narrow entrance to a harbour; dune, a sand beach; barachois, a pond or lagoon at the mouth of a river; *anse*, a cove; and *perdu*, pronounced "bedoo," a cove by a stream. All of these could be found on maps.

Unlike Aboriginal names, New England and Loyalist names generally commemorated either people or places left behind in the homeland or home region. Whereas French naming was more of a dialogue or dialectic with the Aboriginal tradition and maintained the connection with place, English naming, Ganong asserted, was a superimposition. For indigenous people, here as elsewhere, language and land were inseparable, and the characteristics of the latter were recorded in great detail. Few if any English names, on the other hand, describe places or events. Ganong regarded this as evidence of a people accustomed to exercising control and regulating its affairs through courts and councils, not dialogue. Parishes, counties, and blocks of land granted for royal and military service were often named after leading grantees or prominent government and military personnel. Others such as Hampstead, Kingston, Lincoln, and Westfield were simply transplanted place names. In the case of Loyalists, this indicated an affection for the mother country, but the names, especially those with royal associations, were also a reminder to visiting Englishmen of how loyal they had been to the crown and the price they had paid for it. Confederation, Ganong noted, left no record in place nomenclature.

The emigrant tides that swept across the Maritimes from Great Britain in the peace that followed Waterloo deposited a host of Scottish and Irish names. When added to existing names, these produced a place nomenclature more varied and attractive, according to Ganong, than in most new countries. Saint John and the Miramichi in particular began to acquire a decidedly Irish cast. With words and names from at least five languages applied over several centuries, place names were a palimpsest, commemorating nearly every important population movement and most of the men prominent in provincial history. The province's greatest good fortune, Ganong thought, was the bequest of so many Aboriginal names, many of which are melodious and dignified. Among his favourites were Restigouche, Aroostook, Oromocto, Kennebecasis, Patapedia, and Clereustic.

On the question of names and spelling in maps and print, Ganong was a pragmatist. In letters to local newspapers, *Science*, and the naming agency itself, the Geographic Board of Canada, which published its first report in 1902 and its fifteenth in 1917, he complained of the occasional substitution of abstract and academic names for those used locally.

Even before the publication of the 1900 report he had written to Dr. Inch, the New Brunswick representative on the Geographic Board, suggesting, at Inch's request, a number of principles the board might follow in cases of unsettled spelling. Ganong's general recommendation was long usage, euphony, and ease of pronunciation should govern.

In a five-page letter to the board, written in 1905 after the publication of the first report, he arranged, in alphabetical order, examples of change where he considered the board, in not following his recommendation, had been heavy-handed. He began with the change from the euphonious Cains River, pronounced almost as one word, to Cain River, a form he had never seen in print or heard spoken. Likewise, to avoid apostrophes, Mace's Bay became Mace Bay and Deadman's Harbour Deadman Harbour. Frye Island replaced the euphonious Frye's Island, and White Mills replaced White's Mills, implying an erroneous origin. Point de Bute, an English settlement since 1755, became the difficult-to-pronounce Pont à Buot, thought to have been but not proven to be, the original French name. The anglicized form was now so habitual, even among French speakers, that change seemed egregious. Canoose (or Canouse) expressed perfectly the local pronunciation, which its replacement Kanus did not. In Canoose/Canouse the accent is on the second syllable, pronounced so as to rhyme with *moose*, whereas in the proposed change, Kanus, the accent would more likely be on the first. Ganong remarked on the "pure pedantry" of such changes. One wonders what he might have thought of the dropping, in public and official references, of the familiar "Maritimes" in favour of the bureaucratic "Atlantic Canada."

By the 1920s, official mapping agencies had become more sympathetic to local usage and more reconciled to Ganong's defence of it. In 1927 G. A. Bennett, in his first year in charge of the Topographical Survey of Canada, wrote to Ganong to ask for his help in adopting the "best nomenclature"—the most historically accurate and least locally offensive—on the Fredericton and Moncton map sheets. Many of the names, obtained from local residents by the plane tablers in the rush of summer work, needed to be checked. Delighted to oblige, Ganong cited remarkably detailed evidence from documents, old maps, and his own field surveys in the several cases where origins or spellings were unclear. A typical example was his response to a question about Chapel Bar on the St. John River:

Chapel Bar is the one exposed at low summer water, just above Hart's Island, parallel with main shore. It is clearly marked and named on the Foulis map of the River St. John of 1850, and appears in the Bent report of the river of 1836, and is still locally known and used. (Three or four other bars also fall within the limits of your map, of which I can supply the names if the bars appear on your map.) The place is interesting because marking the reputed head of tide (which should also be marked on your map I should think) on the St. John, though I think it runs a little higher on high spring tides.

A few years later the board again asked for his help with the Newcastle and St. Martin's sheets. He also won the argument over Pont à Buot (for Point de Bute) that he had objected to thirty years previously. In the end he and the board compromised, both sides agreeing to Point de Bute. Eight other name changes that Ganong submitted at the same time, in 1935, the board accepted unanimously.

In 1933 the Secretary of the Geographic Board of Canada, J. H. Corry, also asked Ganong if he would check place names and spellings in three forthcoming hydrographic charts of the St. John River below Fredericton. Ganong pointed first to the error of dropping the possessive "s" in several of the names. In nearly all cases, the old form was more euphonic and easier to pronounce, and dropping it especially in cases where the use was invariable induced feelings akin to resentment. A striking case was the proposed elimination of the *s* in Boar's Head, a rust-coloured rock that resembled the head—sloping forehead and upturned snout—of a boar visible from all the river steamers. The replacement, Boar Head, would be comparatively meaningless. He made the point that the arbitrary dismissal of long-established local usages not only raised questions about authenticity but the even larger question of whether a map, professing to be accurate, has any more right to misrepresent the local nomenclature than the local topography: "Is it fair that the people who help pay for the construction of accurate maps should find on them a nomenclature unfamiliar and often grating on their sense of fitness, just because of an arbitrary rule of [a] Geographic Board…which lives in Ottawa."

In a departure from the normal run of questioning, J. H. Corry also drew on Ganong's physiographic knowledge by asking for information about the main stream and tributaries of the Meduxnekeag River in western New Brunswick and northern Maine. He wanted to know which part of the river would be considered the main stream and which names should be used to designate the several branches. He also asked Ganong if he might be able to provide a rough sketch map.

When the new transcontinental railway line was proposed early in the last century, Ganong, concerned that the names for new stations and halts be geographically and historically suitable, in October 1908 wrote to the commissioners with a list of eighteen names that they might consider using. Among them were Lushington, for a station near the Quebec–New Brunswick border, in honour of Sir Stephen Lushington, the final arbiter in the Quebec–New Brunswick border dispute; Wilkinson, for a station north of the Tobique in honour of John Wilkinson, surveyor and author of the first fine map of the province; Negoot (the original name for the Tobique) for a station near or on the river; and Beausoleil, for a station between the Washdemoak and Moncton after a distinguished early Acadian resident of Petitcodiac who befriended English captives despite the hostilities between French and English.

By the late 1920s, at the bidding of Fannie Eckstorm, American mapping agencies were also consulting Ganong about the correct spelling of Aboriginal names. Eckstorm, like Ganong, championed the use of the local and vernacular over the bureaucratic. She had suggested to the Maine Public Utilities Commission that place names on new maps be decided by representatives drawn from the local communities, not pedants and bureaucrats. Her suggestion, forwarded by the commission, won the endorsement of the United States Geographic Board. In a letter to Eckstorm in 1933, it noted where a spelling had been fixed by long usage its policy was not to overturn it in favour of a spelling closer to the original.

When, in that same year, the U.S. Geological Survey asked Ganong to comment upon nomenclature in advance sheets of its Maine maps, he singled out Nicatous for his "unqualified disapproval." The name applied to an important lake and stream whose names, because of their position, would affect more than one map sheet. "The word appearing in

James Vroom. New Brunswick Museum, Ganong Collection: 1987-17-478

the upper right corner…as Nicatous, is properly Nicatowis, accented on the third syllable, and meaning 'the little fork' (of two forks, the lesser one is the idea)." The larger fork was Nicatow, the old name of the Medway, at the junction of the West and East Branches of the Penobscot River. Nicatowis indicated the smaller of two rivers; the distinction was important to Native travellers. The word was always Nicatowis until the early 1880s when changed to Nicatous by Jonathan Darling, the owner of a popular and widely advertised sporting camp, "who simply knew no better." In an indignant response to the Geological Survey, Ganong wrote: "the spelling is vulgar, erroneous, and due wholly to one man's corruption of the word. It ought not to be countenanced any longer." If the USGS required evidence of the historical spelling of the name and the continued use of Nicatowis into the then current century, he could provide chapter and verse. He might have been asked to do so, but the name Nicatous remains.

In spite of his vigilance, Ganong's naming in his own maps and articles did not escape criticism. In 1922 James Vroom, St. Stephen's accomplished town clerk and treasurer, questioned Ganong's dropping of the "blessed word" Magaguadavic (translated as "river of eels") in favour of the then current Magadavie. While not arguing for the inviolability of place names, and as opposed as Ganong was to the Geographic Board's practice of "murdering" old names, Vroom thought that wherever possible official place names, especially richly poetic ones that indicate origins and identity, should be retained. Current spellings and pronunciations were constantly changing, and while many still used Magadavic, as distinct from Macadavie, Vroom was not convinced that the current usage had outgrown the old spelling. As the map-maker and writer Ganong had the whip hand, but Vroom thought the original name should be retained. For his original research and writing on local and natural history the University of New Brunswick granted Vroom an honorary M.A. But the one honour the ultra-modest Vroom coveted, and never received, was membership in the Royal Society of Canada. One small pleasure, that one hopes he was not denied, he expressed in a letter to Ganong in 1928: "I hope sometime to have a day in the fields with you when we can talk over things of mutual interest and recall the pleasures of other days."

THE ORIGINS OF SETTLEMENTS

Like the earlier monographs in the series, this one, too, had no templates or predecessors. Ganong approached the study with the same method and directness that he applied to organic nature. His aim, as in the case of his plant studies, was "to explain why each European settlement in New Brunswick is where it is, and what it is." He named three determining factors: environmental, historical, and racial or cultural. During the initial stages of settlement, environmental factors dominated. For farmers—the majority of the pioneer settlers—good, treeless, or thinly treed soils were crucial. The marshland soils at the head of the bay attracted Acadians, and the intervale, riverine soils of the Saint John valley New Englanders and Loyalists. According to Ganong, a critical physical factor affecting the primary distribution and the ethnic character of settlement was the neck of land that connects the province to peninsular Nova Scotia and closes off the Bay of Fundy. When all long-distance movement was by water, it created two separate avenues of approach to the province. New Englanders and Loyalists came into the Bay of Fundy from the south, and Europeans to the east and north shores from the Atlantic. He attributed the settlement of the Miramichi and the Restigouche, preponderantly by Scots, English, and Irish, to the availability of cheap passage on returning timber vessels. The relative remoteness of the North Shore from the New England and Loyalist settlements also made it attractive to Acadians after their Expulsion from the head of the bay. He regarded the Expulsion (Acadians refused to sign an oath of allegiance to the British, the standard requirement of an occupying power) as a regrettable war measure, a defensive rather than a vindictive action. Without the security of the oath the British, Ganong insisted, feared they were harbouring an enemy within. He attributed the Acadians' settlement of the north shore to the region's isolation and relative safety from the English in the south.

Secondary distributions he attributed to cultural differences. Accustomed to braving unsettled territory and less tied to place and community than other groups, New Englanders moved into the woods and onto solitary islands, building settlements that were small and scattered rather than compact and centralized. English and Scots on the other hand, having crossed an ocean to an unknown land and having come from regions of compact villages, tended to stick together. Nucleation was most pronounced in Acadian settlements, where custom, language, religion, and the hostility of Anglophones encouraged togetherness. Ganong also thought pioneering and the "racial character" of the French were not a good match. While they made good explorers and adventurers, he posited, the French lacked the strong individualism and passion for material prosperity necessary to good pioneers. The French peasantry were home-loving and sociable, and as devout Catholics they were strongly attached to the church and their church-centred agricultural villages. In regions of Acadian settlement, there was no broad fringe of pioneer outposts characteristic of the Anglo-Saxon communities.

As to the future of settlement, Ganong was optimistic. He was confident the tendency of immigrants to bypass the Maritimes was temporary. Once the fertile areas of the west had been filled, immigrants would look once again to New Brunswick and the east. Settlement would expand not only into the north of the province, but under careful and scientific systems of cultivation it would fill up areas in the centre and the south now seen as unprofitable. With water power and vast forest resources, Ganong was on safer ground and believed the woods, if properly managed, would be productive again despite the historic depredations. He had no doubt the enormous power of the Fundy tides would one day be harnessed and promote manufacturing.

With his love of inventory and attention to detail, Ganong followed this general survey of the settlement with an alphabetical listing of all the settlements in the province, accompanied by a brief sketch of each and references to any printed sources of information concerning it. There are 757 entries, ranging in length from a few lines to several paragraphs, and filling 70 pages. Related to this was his postmaster survey, conducted the previous year, that consisted of a printed questionnaire, sent to every postmaster in the province as well as interested individuals, requesting information on local history ranging from the names of early settlers to noteworthy events and place names. To those able to assist, he sent sketch maps asking them to identify former settlements, older names, roads, trails, Aboriginal camps, and historic sites. It was yet another demonstration of his mantra: facts first, theory and interpretation later.

As an historian, Ganong's instincts were antiquarian. He was more comfortable with empirical evidence—the material objects and measurable details of the settlements—than with speculation about what these signified. Accumulated facts, however, do not make a history. His passion was for particulars, not abstractions or generalizations. When his friend John Clarence Webster offered to nominate him as a candidate for the Royal Society's Tyrrell Gold Medal in History in 1929, Ganong objected; he was not interested in awards and his was not the kind of history that interested the society. Webster, who had already sounded several prominent fellows, persisted, and Ganong, over his initial objection, accepted the award in 1931.

Yet his immediate reaction to Webster's offer was probably sound. Ganong was a historian only in a narrow sense. He had no gift, as he readily acknowledged, for writing compelling, narrative history. His ideal history, as he declared in his monograph on the origins of settlements, would consist of a firm skeleton of facts and analysis "clothed in the graceful draperies" of a stirring narrative. The facts and analysis he could provide, but not the stirring or engaging narrative. As an empiricist, he was at ease only with what could be seen, touched, and measured: shorelines, boundaries, maps, settlements, the objects and features of the tangible and visible world. This, as D. C. Harvey, Provincial Archivist for Nova Scotia, would point out in a paper in the 1940s, wasn't the kind of history that Maritimers needed. The then current need, as he saw it, was for papers, articles, and books on the post-Confederation Maritime economy and on the economic, social, and cultural adjustments required in a world whose colonial underpinnings had been removed.

The First Nations, Acadian, and Loyalist ground, Harvey asserted, had been thoroughly worked over by Ganong and others, and the returns were marginal. As a botanist and natural scientist first, Ganong had little feel for political, economic, or social discourse. His gifts to the province were his ecological studies, translations, his work on boundaries, nomenclature, and mapping, and, yet to be considered, the detailed hands-on fieldwork he conducted every summer along its rivers and shores and in the remote and wild places of the interior that had never been studied and in some cases never explored. His objective on these annual explorations was to fill in the blank and poorly defined areas in the provincial map and shed light on the processes that had determined the build or the physiography of the province.

Chapter 5

⁓⊘ℂ ℂ⊘⁓

EXPLORATIONS

E very summer except for his two "mighty homesick" years in
Germany and the summer his son was born (1924), Ganong
explored part or parts of New Brunswick—on foot, by canoe,
wagon, bicycle, and finally by car and caravan. His base was either his
sister's house or her summer cottage in Rothesay, on the Kennebecasis
a few miles above Saint John. Susan B. Ganong, or "Suzie" as her family
knew her, was principal and owner of Netherwood, a private girls' school
in Rothesay. Ganong's main objective on these summer excursions was to
fill blank areas in the physiographic and topographic maps of the province.
Physiography is the bones and musculature of the land, the underlying
formations of which topography, the surface features, are the expression.
Geology, the rocks the bones are made of, had been studied, but the physiography, except in some of the settled, accessible southern regions, hardly
at all. Although understood in a very general way, little had been written
about it, and most of this had been incidental to the study of the geology.
In a manuscript report on physiography, Ganong cited in particular the
geological writings of L. W. Bailey, his mentor in natural sciences at UNB.

The general physiography of New Brunswick is controlled by three
highland ranges, the worn-down ends of the Appalachian system that
enter the province from the southwest and trend northeast toward the

Gulf of St. Lawrence. Except for the main branch of the St. John River, they determine the general alignment of the rivers and the bays and serve as watersheds that separate the river systems. Although described as highlands, the interior and north of New Brunswick is an ancient peneplain, a surface levelled by eons of erosion that was subsequently uplifted and into which rivers have cut deeply. It is only hilly where converging streams have cut the plateau-like surface into fragments or where occasional masses of harder rocks have been more resistant to erosion than their surroundings.

Ganong divided the river systems into three groups: the Fundian, emptying southeastward into the Bay of Fundy; the Chaleurian, emptying eastward and northward into Chaleur Bay; and the Northumbrian, emptying northeastward into the Gulf of St. Lawrence. The great anomalous river is the St. John. Like its tributary, the Tobique, it must once have obeyed the general southwest–northeast trend and flowed into Chaleur Bay, but uplift of the peneplain to the north and east, Ganong surmised, caused its waters to pool up, possibly as a vast lake, and when a critical level had been reached, they escaped southward across the major grain of the country, toward the Bay of Fundy.

While acknowledging that a division of the province into river systems might be the most useful for charting its life and history, Ganong thought a more natural one, that took account of both the geology and accompanying topography, might be one based upon the general configuration of the surface. He identified four divisions, still recognized by the Geological Survey of Canada. First, a northern plateau region, in effect, a great peneplain 243–300 metres above sea level, of Upper Silurian rocks with Lower Carboniferous rocks around its edges. Below this is a central highland region of ancient granites and slates, arranged in a series of irregular ridges that run from the middle and upper St. Croix to Chaleur Bay. They culminate in a district of high hills, from 610 to 820 metres above sea level, between the headwaters of the Tobique, the Nepisiguit, and the Miramichi. The highest of them, Mount Carleton at 820 metres, is the highest point in the province. East of the central highlands is a peneplain, high in the west but low and level in the east, of Carboniferous and Lower Carboniferous sandstones. Ganong's fourth

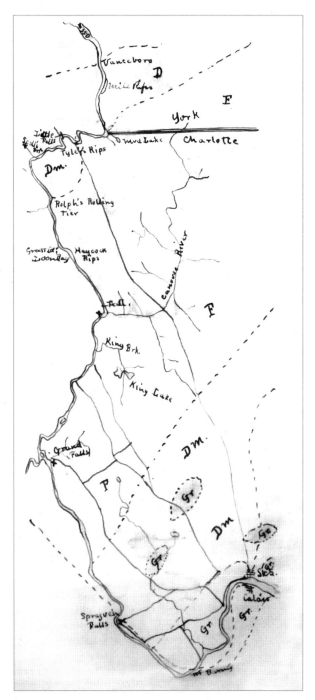

Ganong's sketch map of the St. Croix River in western Charlotte County, the locale of his early inland explorations. NEW BRUNSWICK MUSEUM, GANONG COLLECTION: F455-16V

division is a 48-kilometre–wide southern belt of highlands and ridges, reaching heights of 426 metres, following the line of the Bay of Fundy between St. Stephen and Moncton. Built of ancient hard felsite and granite, they are exceedingly broken, cut by rivers into a series of hills, ridges, and plateaus. In the far west they protrude as islands in Passamaquoddy Bay. In the east they fall off to sea level at the Petitcodiac.

As well as accenting the physiography, the rivers were the sole avenues through the virtually impenetrable forest and into the largely unsettled and inaccessible centre and north of the province, J. W. Bailey's "Great New Brunswick Wilderness." If equipment was needed, the canoe was the only effective means of getting it there. As a system, the rivers were accommodating. Their coverage of the province was comprehensive and only a few presented insurmountable obstacles to the expert and determined canoeist. One portage only was needed to navigate the entire length of the St. John above the falls at its mouth, while, as Ganong pointed out, an experienced canoeist could descend the Restigouche, the Southwest Miramichi, Cains, Salmon, Canaan, Tobique, and many other principal streams without a carry. Few of the rivers had been surveyed or mapped, and some had hardly been explored, traversed only by solitary sportsmen and by lumbermen running lines to estimate amounts of standing timber. For rivers that were known, published maps often gave a misleading impression of their relative sizes, partly because their headwaters were rarely shown and partly because of their representation by single or double lines that reflected not the size of the rivers but the extent to which they were known and used. Many of the small headwater and tributary streams, too, were not navigable by canoe in the usual sense. Even in fair water, only a light one-person canoe shod with cedar splints for dragging it over rocks might negotiate them. In streams in the centre and south of the province, low water in late summer could also make navigation difficult. Camp equipment had to be reduced to a minimum, and the canoeist had to be willing and able to wade, lift, and haul.

Ganong's ambition was to examine every navigable stream, work out its physiographic history, and do as much topographical mapping and sketching as he could. There had been no province-wide topographical survey, and such detailed mapping as had been done was patchy

Hauling up Eel River.

Our sail on Grand Lake

Portage over Mile Rips.

Poachers fleeing from game wardens

A selection of hand-drawn cartoons from Ganong's diminutive early field notebooks. The mature Ganong was less playful. NEW BRUNSWICK MUSEUM, GANONG COLLECTION (TOP TO BOTTOM): F455-15G, F455-16C, F455-19B, F455-20I

and often inaccurate. Add to this the general ignorance of the size and depth of lakes and the elevation of prominent hills and the topographic map was decidedly threadbare. Ganong aimed to repair at least some of this. For most, the task would have been Sisyphean, but for Ganong it was another avocation. After "a good many years of loving study," he wrote in 1927, he had canoed down virtually every navigable river and stream in the province and poled his way up a great many of them. He published his findings as short studies of river and lake systems in the *Bulletin* of NHSNB. His intention had been to record his observations

More cartoons, accenting Ganong's notebooks. Top–bottom: The mishap with Sam Kain; Mohawk canoe party. NEW BRUNSWICK MUSEUM, GANONG COLLECTION: F455-16K, F455-18K

and publish them as occasional papers in the *Bulletin*. He had no conception of how the work would grow. He began in 1896 with general observations on physiography and followed these with systematic studies of the lake and river basins under the heading of "Notes on the Natural History and Physiography of New Brunswick." There were 138 of these. His first study was of the basin of the Lepreau, in 1898. Other reports followed annually, usually with several entries in one year, and ended in 1917 with a report on the physiography of the west branch of the South Branch of the Nepisiguit. Forty-five of the 75 entries on physiography

Ganong's meeting with a self-important cleric, a former UNB classmate. New Brunswick Museum, Ganong Collection: F455-20A

and topography were on rivers alone. After the demise of the *Bulletin* in 1917 Ganong published, at his own expense, additional reports in six facsimile issues, binding, numbering, and paging them so as to replicate the defunct journal.

For each of the major rivers and their tributaries, Ganong sketched their physiographic histories, explaining for Society members and *Bulletin* readers how the composition and structure of the underlying rocks, millions of years of erosion and subsequent uplift, and the last ice age had determined the direction of the rivers, the shape of their valleys, and the gradient of their beds. "In the whole of the attractive science of physiography," he wrote, "there is no subject of greater importance or interest than the changes which river valleys undergo in the course of their evolution. Rivers are forever extending their basins and moving their watersheds, while frequently they capture other rivers. Hence it comes about that some rivers are composites of two or more streams originally separate. A river with a simple uneventful history would possess a fairly direct general course, a drainage basin of somewhat regular outline, and a valley increasing in width and decreasing in slope from source to mouth."

Few rivers, however, follow this pattern. Varying resistances to erosion in the underlying rocks, movement and faulting in the earth's crust, and just yesterday in terms of geologic time, masses of ice moving across the landscape and on melting releasing and sometimes dumping indiscriminately their massive loads of silt, sand, gravel, and boulders, caused rivers to change course. Often, too, the rivers themselves were responsible for deviations from the straight and narrow path. Like immeasurably slow-moving saws, the headwaters of rivers work their way backwards into the highlands from which they spring, capturing and diverting the waters of less aggressive streams as they do so. The result is changes in direction that nothing else can explain. Ganong's prime example was the Nepisiguit. Twice in its course it makes right-angle bends and flows though a valley that for most of its length lessens in breadth and increases in slope toward its mouth. The irregularities point to a complicated history. To explain it, Ganong submitted that the Nepisiguit is a composite of three other rivers: "a small portion of the Tobique system, a very large part from the Upsalquitch system, [and] a part from the Miramichi system." Only the lower course, according to Ganong, is the true original Nepisiguit. Working its way back at its head, it gradually captured and made tributary to itself parts of the other systems.

The remarkable right angles of the Miramichi rivers, which come together below Boiestown to form a single, evenly flowing trunk, Ganong attributed to the warping and faulting of an older gently sloping peneplain down which they flowed independently to the sea, throwing them together. The Main Southwest Miramichi is second in size and importance only to the St. John. To sort out the remarkably rough and complicated courses of the branches of the river above Boiestown required many weeks of study over three summers. Although willing to speculate in cases where there was little hard evidence, he described himself chiefly

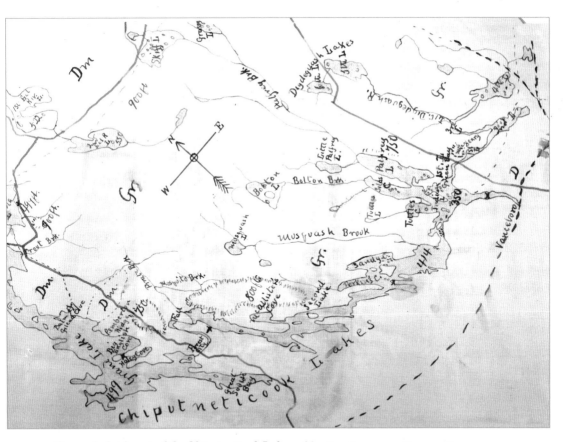

Ganong's sketch map of the Chiputneticook Lakes, 1887. NEW BRUNSWICK MUSEUM, GANONG COLLECTION: F455-16H

A perilous downhill portage. Going downhill with a brakeless wagon could be much more difficult than going up. New Brunswick Museum, Ganong Collection: F455-18d

as a fact-finder and insisted that any hypotheses advanced on the scanty data he could provide should be regarded as tentative. Advanced theory could wait. But if the hypotheses prompted others to research then his purpose would have been served.

Ganong's annual explorations during his years at Harvard and Smith were carefully planned to investigate some aspect of the physiography and topography of the province. In fact, however, they tended to be multipurpose. If travelling in inhabited country, he gathered information on place names, portage routes, and the cultural and settlement history of the places he passed through. Few Aboriginal or resident Europeans he encountered escaped his questioning—his "ruling passion," as he once described it. Only visiting sport fishermen and hunters, who had nothing to offer him, were safe. A canoe trip tended to be a succession of base camps from which excursions, sometimes days in length, were made on foot (packing trips) to add detail to or correct a map, measure heights with an aneroid barometer, take angles and sight lines with a compass and telescopic alidade, or examine some aspect of the physiography or topography. He kept a detailed daily journal of each journey, in diminutive script in small notebooks, on which this account is based. When finished he pasted the entries onto the pages of a bound journal now in the safekeeping of the New Brunswick Museum. There are more than eighty entries. He planned to write a book about them, but he ran out of time.

Chapter 6

EARLY JOURNEYS

Ganong's first camping excursions were for pleasure and for fishing. He began locally but soon ventured inland. He was a skilled small-boat handler, canoeist, and camper. His first overnight camping excursion was from Carleton, in west Saint John, in late June 1880, when he was sixteen: "We were started [for Clinches Stream, Musquash] at last. An ordinary horse, a fine easy phaeton, and three of us off for a day's fishing on the Musquash. First there was Charles Brown, my uncle, the originator of our expedition, Fred Brittani, another uncle of mine, and myself." Then followed pages of pencilled notes with details of the twenty-four-kilometre journey, the camp, and fishing. The very early morning, after a few hours' sleep in a makeshift camp, "was glorious. Not a ripple on the water, not a sound save the noise of the oars and the melodious croaking of the bullfrogs. No sign of civilization on the banks, only the calm silent forest and the notes of the birds awakening to the pleasures of another day. Everything so calm, so peaceful, so unlike the noisy city from which we had come; how beautiful it looked. The sky reddening with the rising sun, the water so still, without a ripple." The pattern was set: Ganong's enthusiasm and note taking never wavered.

On the expeditions that followed he collected specimens and made nature notes. In August 1882 he, a younger brother, and two friends sailed down to the mouth of the St. Croix River into Passamaquoddy Bay. The personnel in order of rank were: W. F. Ganong, captain and cook; S. W. Kain, mate; Robert Stevens; and E. J. Ganong. Sam Kain, a classmate at UNB, was a frequent companion on his early excursions. When near St. Andrews, Ganong noted: "I made a sketch of the peculiar geology of the place and then went to get water. At the spring I captured a sort of lizard…I have it now preserved in alcohol." He also made references to conglomerate rocks in a cave and crystallized rock from the trap rock that formed the bar between St. Andrews and adjacent Minister's Island. Before the excursion, Loring Bailey, Ganong's professor at UNB, had suggested he look for fossils that might help to explain the geology of Passamaquoddy Bay. Although Ganong and his crew failed to find fossils, he did return with a profound interest in the natural features of that region. On subsequent boat and camping trips on the shore and near islands of Passamaquoddy, Ganong studied the geology as well as the botany and zoology. His chief interests then were zoological and botanical.

For the "down river" trip in a small sailboat from St. Stephen in the summer of 1883 the "Dramatis Personae" were: W. F. Ganong, senior at UNB, captain, and cook; Samuel W. Kain, now at the Customs House in Saint John; Ganong's younger brother, Edwin, preparing to enter UNB; and Harry M. Wetmore, an employee of Ganong Bros, the now well known candy company based in St. Stephen. The following summer, Ganong had promoted Sam Kain to botanist and himself to captain, geologist, and zoologist. His brother, Edwin, was appointed cook and Harry Wetmore assistant cook. As young scientists, not just adventurers, he and Kain carried a "scientific box" containing everything needed for scientific work "on a small scale"—reference books, compass, alcohol for preserving specimens, sealed bottles, etc. Ganong enjoyed the company of friends but he had already developed a taste for solo travel that would prove to be life-long. In 1885 he wrote of the relief of getting away from home, "as of the lifting of a great load," when setting off from the St. Stephen wharf for a sailing and camping trip around Passamaquoddy Bay. As the boat left the wharf his spirit soared with the breeze that sprang up astern and at the sight of the great placid river and the freedom of movement it promised.

Earlier that summer he made his first trip to the interior with Sam Kain. They paddled through the chain of Squatook and Temiscouata lakes in Quebec then down the Madawaska and the St. John to Fredericton. Kain would describe the trip in the *American Canoeist*. They travelled north to Edmundston by train, and to negotiate a damaged and weakened railway bridge south of the city they hired a railway trolley and strapped the canoe on top, a manoeuvre they would adopt again to avoid rough water. A horse-drawn wagon took them twenty-five kilometres up the Madawaska River,

"Down River"

Being an account of a two weeks trip among the Islands and Rivers of Charlotte Co. New Brunswick, during the Summer of 1883.

Written and enlarged from notes taken during the trip, at the University of New Brunswick by the Captain

Dramatis Personae

Wm. F. Ganong: Senior of the University of U.B. Captain and Cook. St. Stephen

Samuel W. Kain: Formerly student of U.N.B. Employée of Custom House St. John

Edwin J. Ganong: Student preparing for the U.N.B. St. Stephen

Harry M. Wetmore: Employée of Ganong Bros. St. Stephen

1883

Captain Ganong's cast of players in his downriver expedition, 1883. NEW BRUNSWICK MUSEUM, GANONG COLLECTION: F455-6A

and then a lighter buggy, that the driver called a "catamaran," took them across a portage to their starting point, Muddy Lake. The driver warned them to beware of a little "smart" water on their circuitous route back to the St. John. The canoe aside, their heaviest piece of equipment was a nine-pound "A" tent. Although both were skilled canoeists a stretch of smart ("seething, foaming") water on their approach to Lake Temiscouata undid them, overturning the canoe and sweeping away provisions, clothing, and money. They rescued the canoe and good (French) Samaritans from a village on Lake Temiscouata provided enough food and cash for them to continue down the Madawaska to Edmundston.

Sam Kain also accompanied Ganong on his first systematic physiographic study: an "eagerly anticipated" trip up-country to the Cheputnicook Lakes and then back to Milltown and St. Stephen in August 1887. "The day of our 'Chepedneck' trip has come at last—dawning this morning clear, cool, and bright as new wine," he wrote in his journal. "This

For Ganong, transcendence was a month-long wilderness journey with a strong, woods-loving companion, each with his own light canoe, sounding every lake, climbing every mountain, and doing so slowly. The favoured route was up the Tobique from Perth, into the central highlands, and down the Nepisiguit to Bathurst. He did this in 1889. NEW BRUNSWICK MUSEUM, GANONG COLLECTION: F455-27C

day looked forward to by Sam and myself for a year—written about, talked about, thought about, dreamed about, and here it is at last." They went up the Eel River from Benton, through the Chiputneticook Lakes and down the St. Croix to Milltown along rivers so filled with logs that obliging river drivers had to clear a way for them. On Grand Lake, Sam held a small birch tree in the box for a sail. Ganong made delicate coloured sketch maps of the lakes and, to illustrate their misadventures, cartoon-like drawings. They were a hardy pair. The heavy rains, frequent portages, and rough stretches of water that required lowering the canoe by rope, failed to dismay them. The true canoeist and camper, declared the determined twenty-three-year-old Ganong, is undeterred by discomfort and takes pleasure in ignoring it.

For short portages around falls and rapids they carried the canoe, and for a particularly long one they balanced it on a buckboard. To take the canoe down to Baring they hired another rail trolley. Downriver from Baring to Milltown the St. Croix in places was so thick with loose and rafted logs that they had to roll the canoe across them. That day they lunched on "a wing of logs," and the following evening a lumberman invited them to the camp for dinner. Thus ended, Ganong wrote with evident satisfaction, the trip of 1887, "the best trip we ever had." He and Sam had travelled about 200 kilometres by water and completed "some fair scientific work."

Marriage to Jean Murray (Muriel) Carman in the spring of 1889 did not disrupt Ganong's summer routine. Early that summer he canoed with his bride down the St. John from Edmundston to Fredericton. In August, after high summer in Cambridge, Massachusetts, he was back on the upper St. John River at Madawaska with Sam Kain.

Cambridge is hardly a grim mill town, but Ganong, like the poet John Keats, had been "city-kempt" too long. He also wilted in New England's hot, humid summers, writing later in letters to his friend G. R. F. Prowse in Winnipeg how much he enjoyed every minute of the occasional almost-Arctic winters, taking a long daily walk no matter how strong the cold. Constant heat and humidity sapped the energy of his "Eskimo" temperament: "I like cold and especially very cold and snowy weather best of all," he wrote. In a January 1925 letter from Northampton to his sister Sue at

Rothesay he complained that by missing temperatures of 55° below zero (Fahrenheit) at Edmundston and 42° below at Chatham, he felt cheated of his birthright. He described the cool summer of 1936 as "the greatest summer ever—cool all summer—even cold at times." Each year he delighted in his escape to cool-temperate New Brunswick: "So here we are in the midst of the loveliness of the Upper St. John—outdoors in the land so long wished for, thought of and talked of. It all seemed too good to ever come here—when looked at from the toil and heat of Cambridge. Yet here it has come, and so far it is all our fancies painted."

Ganong poling down the Aroostook Gorge, 1897. New Brunswick Museum, Ganong Collection: 1987-17-1218-37

A year later he and Sam canoed down the Southwest Miramichi from the forks east of Foreston to Newcastle. Ethnography might have been the focus. The highlight of that trip was his meeting with Newell Paul, a well-informed Mi'kmaq. Aboriginal poachers who came to one of their camps explained the technique of salmon spearing by torchlight so colourfully that they hoped to be invited to go along but were too law-abiding to ask. En route to Newcastle they talked for hours to Aboriginals and older European residents about their personal and settlement histories. One morning on Beaubears Island Ganong walked four kilometres to interview John O'Neill, a hermit with a literary reputation. His library, Ganong noted wryly, was limited to a few law books, but he knew a great deal about the old settlers and the history of the settlement. At the Eel Ground reserve, near Newcastle, Ganong also talked at length with the Mi'kmaq chief Tom Barnaby, who described a settlement that stretched for two miles along the river. Each house had cleared ground around it designed, in vain it would appear, for farming. Barnaby alleged bitterly that Moses Perley, the Indian agent at the time, had sold their band or tribal lands, except for the riverside reserve, and that they had received nothing for them. At the same settlement Ganong and Kain talked to an old Mi'kmaw woman who had lost ten children from consumption and now lived alone, attended only by a young girl. The woman remembered when the Mi'kmaq had lived in bark wigwams, not houses.

On his return from his two-year stint in Germany in the summer of 1895, Ganong immediately took to the waters. A major consolation in Germany had been comparing, always unfavourably, German and New Brunswick rivers as waterways for canoeing. In 1895 Ganong came down the Magaguadavic with his brother Arthur, and in 1896 he canoed, possibly alone, down the Restigouche. In 1897, with Sam Kain, two brothers, and a cousin, Ganong spent two weeks surveying the Mahood lakes and Lepreau Basin in Charlotte County. No other part of the province so near to settlements was so little known, and probably no stream carrying an equal volume of water was so difficult for canoe navigation. The bed was rough, slippery, and boulder strewn, and even at fair water it took two long days of "the severest labour" and twenty portages to cover the eight miles from its outlet at Lake Victoria to the North Branch.

The surroundings were also daunting, or would have been to most voyagers. Large areas of timber flattened by the 1869 Saxby Gale were prey to such strong fires that even the soil had been burnt and washed away, exposing a wasteland of granite boulders. His report on the Lepreau in the 1898 *Bulletin* was the first of his planned publications on physiography.

In 1899 Ganong and his brother Arthur with "a birch canoe apiece" went to the forks of the Tobique (a tributary of the St. John), poled up the little Tobique, portaged to the Nepisiguit, and then canoed down it to Bathurst. En route, Ganong surveyed and mapped—he was the first to do so—Nictau or "Little Tobique" Lake. He thought it the loveliest in the entire province and that it ought to be a provincial park. "Happy is he," he would write in his *Bulletin* account of the physiography, "who, from the ideal camping place upon the island, can watch day after day these beautiful hills in their varying lights and colours, and can know they are his own." He named the highest peak Mount Carleton after Thomas Carleton, the province's first lieutenant governor. In 1928, when asked by the New Brunswick Fish and Game Protective Association to

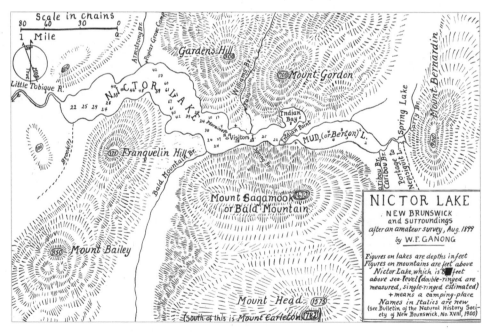

Ganong's map of Nictor Lake, using hachures to indicate the direction and degree of slope, 1899. NEW BRUNSWICK MUSEUM, GANONG COLLECTION: F448-40

recommend a site for a national park, Ganong first outlined the desired scenic, recreational, and wildlife attributes of such a park and then recommended the Mount Carleton–Nictau–Nepisiguit Lake region, "incomparably superior" to any of the other suggested sites. "It is much the most elevated...and therefore has the most suitable summer climate; it is much the most rugged and has the wildest and most distinctively differentiated scenery; it has charming rivers readily navigable for canoes, and many lakes, including the most beautiful lake in the province." To these attributes he added the best trout fishing in New Brunswick, fine forests of both evergreen and hardwood trees, abundant game animals, trails for hiking and camping, and no settlements. Mount Carleton was eventually designated a provincial park in 1970 but the Bay of Fundy, with its clear attraction to tourists, won the national park stakes in 1948. Ganong's ideal park would have been for active provincials first, hurried motorized tourists second.

Chapter 7

THE GREAT NEW BRUNSWICK WILDERNESS

Although his brothers were willing cooks and Sam Kain an accomplished and enthusiastic naturalist, Ganong's post-Munich expeditions into the centre and north of the province featured a change in personnel. Weeks-long expeditions probably ruled out Sam Kain, who would have been tied to his work at the customs office, as well as Ganong's brothers who generously provided "locomotary power" but did not share his deeper interests. His new regular companions were George Upham Hay, teacher, writer, botanist, and president and vice-president of the Natural History Society; Mauran I. Furbish, a map-maker and manufacturer of fishing lines from Attleboro, Massachusetts; and Arthur Henry Pierce, a bachelor colleague from Smith College and a keen outdoorsman. Pierce's background was similar to Ganong's. Born in Massachusetts in 1867, he studied at Amherst and Harvard (for his Ph.D.) and then for six years at the universities of Berlin, Strasbourg, and Paris. At Smith he was Professor of Psychology.

In late July 1895 Ganong and George Upham Hay canoed down the Restigouche from the headwaters to Campbellton on Chaleur Bay. It was a twelve-day journey along a river Hay regarded as the most romantic and picturesque river in a province replete with them. Hay published his account of the journey in the *Bulletin*, noting they had found eleven plants new to the province and several others that were rare or little known before. Although known to sportsmen and a few artists, for naturalists the Restigouche was uncharted territory. In his 1899 presidential address to the NHSNB Hay would echo Ganong, appealing for a comprehensive provincial topographical survey.

From above St. Leonard, on the St. John River, three men with a stout wagon and two horses took their canoe and baggage to the head-waters of the Restigouche. For the first nineteen kilometres of the forty-kilometre journey, Hay and Ganong brought up the rear in a light wagon. For the remaining twenty-one kilometres, they followed on foot over a rough road. Once they had begun the descent, camping was also

Portage with horse team and wagon, Victoria County, 1900. NEW BRUNSWICK MUSEUM, GANONG COLLECTION: 1987-17-1219-2

testing. Tempted one evening by the smoothness of a sand beach they set up their tent only to be savaged by mosquitoes, blackflies, and sand-flies. From then on they retreated to the woods, preferably to slightly elevated sites, closed the tent tight, and built two or three large fires near the tent door. Hay's advice for a satisfactory camping trip was: never sleep on a sand beach, close the tent early, and keep good hours. The river itself, although turbulent, was less troublesome. Ganong had the "unerring instincts" of an expert steersman and never once did they even approach a mishap.

For Hay, the most interesting topographical feature on the Restigouche was Cross Point, "a rocky, dizzy height," surmounted by a wooden cross that towers over ninety metres above the river. At the point, the river

Ganong recording the day's events in one of his field notebooks, 1901. New Brunswick Museum, Ganong Collection: 1987-17-1218-138

doubles back on itself, flowing first to the northeast and then turning so sharply that from the narrow crest an observer can sit, according to Hay, dangling a leg over each channel.

As they passed the mouth of the Upsalquitch, a tributary of the Restigouche and the province's only major northward flowing river, Hay and Ganong resolved to ascend it the following summer and then descend the Tobique to Andover on the St. John. Ganong and others attributed the dominantly southerly direction of the province's rivers to the tendency of the southward advancing, northward retreating ice sheet to dam up the northward flowing rivers and send their waters in the opposite direction. Low water on the Upsalquitch, however, forced a change of plan. Ganong and Hay decided instead to pole up the Nepisiguit and then go down the Tobique to the St. John. They left Bathurst in early August with a four weeks' supply of provisions carried over a rough wagon road to Grand Falls, some thirty-three kilometres upriver. In deference to the fearsome reputation of the Nepisiguit, they bought an extra canoe and hired two Aboriginal guides to take them through or around the rough sections. To negotiate a narrow gorge with rough water about six kilometres from the start, they carried most of the gear around it but entrusted the rest to the two guides who had insisted on poling through the rapids. The canoe capsized and its contents went either to the bottom or floated downstream. They managed to rescue some ham, butter, pork, and fishing tackle but baked beans and all the cooking utensils were lost. They sacked the guides and Ganong never used guides again. While Ganong continued to pole upstream, Hay had to return on foot to the fishing lodge at Grand Falls to replace the lost supplies and gear.

As the more experienced canoeist, Ganong generously offered to do all the poling while Hay botanized. After some persuasion, Hay accepted the offer, but the current was so strong and in places the bed so boulder-strewn that after two days he recanted and took up the bow pole. Freshet ice had made every shrub and bush point downstream, so on narrow stretches of water the canoeists had to combat vegetation as well as current. When the current was too strong for poling or the rocks dangerous, they hauled the canoe upstream by rope. At the headwaters they portaged to the Tobique and then went down to Andover on the St. John.

George Upham Hay writing notes c. 1900. Ganong—in the background—is making camp. NEW BRUNSWICK MUSEUM, GANONG COLLECTION: 1987-17-1218-115

Far from being dismayed by the constant struggle, Hay was enchanted. He described the mood of their camp above Indian Falls near the headwaters of the Nepisiguit: "A spirit of contentment is in the air. The coffee never gave out a more delightful aroma. The flapjacks as they were deftly turned in the air came down in the right place in the frying pan and lay sizzlingly contented with a well-browned surface—done to a charm. We enjoyed with the high spirits of boyhood; the charm of outdoor life in the wilderness." Even hours-long portages around rapids or between streams were among "the delightful troubles of a journey in the wilderness." First they moved their baggage, then tied their coats around the narrow benches at the bow and stern of the canoe, turned the vessel over, and hoisted it bottom up onto their shoulders, "Indian style."

The summer of 1900 found them on the south Tobique lakes—a cluster of eighteen lakes supplying both the Tobique and Miramichi River systems. To them, Ganong applied the ancient Maliseet name "Negoot." The largest of them are Long Lake, Trousers Lake (owing to its distinctive shape), Portage, Adder, and Serpentine. Hay botanized and Ganong surveyed and mapped. For the four-week trip they packed three hundred

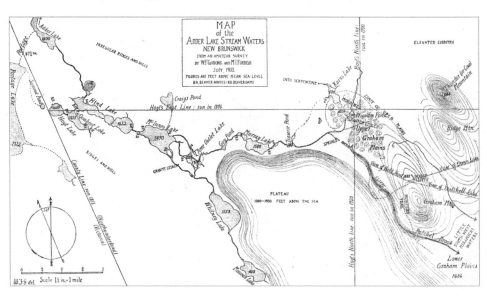

Ganong's map of the Adder Lake stream waters, July 1902. New Brunswick Museum, Ganong Collection: 1987-17-1221-92

pounds of equipment into a sixty-pound basswood canoe, and when they moved camp they had to do so "Klondike style," moving the gear in stages and going back for more.

On the trip they met up with Mauran I. Furbish, a map-maker from Attleboro Falls, and his guide whom Ganong had met in the woods the year before. The two groups worked together, and in early August of the following year, 1901, Ganong and Furbish met at Newburg Junction above Woodstock and from there went to Plaster Rock. Canoe and gear were then portaged over two days, Ganong and Furbish walking (sleeping in a hay barn and a lumber camp) to Long Lake. Then, after more than a week of surveying and guided by the traces of an old (pine) lumber

Ganong surveying with a plane table, Long Lake, 1901. New Brunswick Museum, Ganong Collection: 1987-17-1218-129

road, they cut a path and portaged their outfit sixteen kilometres to Big Lake of the Tuadook group. They then descended the "rough little sw Miramichi" to the main Southwest Miramichi and then to Newcastle.

The Tuadook lake region is remote, "extremely difficult of access," and although visited by a handful of hunters and sketched by surveyors running timber lines, had never been mapped or studied. Ganong and Furbish spent several days there in August 1901 at the camp of Henry Braithwaite, the "prince" of New Brunswick guides and woodsmen, whose intimate knowledge of the topography, plants, and wildlife Ganong hoped might be published for safekeeping. He and Furbish surveyed with a plane table and a hand-held prismatic compass, drawing sketch maps, sounding the lakes, measuring heights with an aneroid barometer,

Final clear-up near Newcastle with unidentified children in the background.
New Brunswick Museum, Ganong Collection: 1987-17-1219-105

roughing in contours, naming unnamed features, and making traverses of any roads they came across. A two-man surveying party, in effect. On the portages between lakes and from the lakes to the Little Southwest Miramichi, sleeping bags were their only cover, and at the end of the portage they brushed out a path, taking two days to cover three miles. They then went back for the canoe and their gear. Ganong confessed that he enjoyed the "legitimized destructiveness" of the cutting. On reaching Big Lake at the end of the portage they were hugely disappointed to find the fresh footprints and a canvas canoe, evidently in use, of two lone hunters and fishermen. They thought they had the wilderness to themselves. The two men, however, who were in awe of the labour of the portages from the Tobique to the Little Southwest Miramichi, were most agreeable, and Ganong, as was his habit, pumped them for information. In spite of his general avoidance of sportsmen, he recorded that there were no two men in New Brunswick whom he would rather have met in the woods.

After making surveys on Big Lake, Ganong and Furbish embarked on the last leg of the trip: the journey down the little known and misleadingly named Little Southwest Miramichi, a far larger river than its name implies and notorious as the most unruly river in New Brunswick. The channel is rough and narrow, and its devious course is a succession of boulder rips and deadwater stretches, requiring wading, dragging, and portaging of the heavier equipment. The going improved after passing the junction of the North Pole Branch, but log jams slowed them and their provisions were almost exhausted, reducing them to a diet of beans, buckwheat, virtually inedible (salty) pea soup, and sugarless tea and coffee. Candles too, were gone, and Ganong had to write his daily notes by firelight. Yet however testing, Ganong described it as "Ye Flawlesse Trippe." They reached Beaubears Island on August 31 and Newcastle on Labour Day.

Ganong admired Furbish, but in his field journal Furbish is simply "F," with no overt references to his character or competence other than his ability to cast standing up in the canoe. On one occasion Ganong, while Furbish was fishing, unthinkingly reached out for a branch and both men, the canoe propelled by the current slipping under them, ended up in the water. The canoe overturned, but their surveying instruments—which, as professionals, they kept in a waterproof bag—were not damaged. Ganong was distraught, but Furbish was simply amused. William J. Long, an American author of animal stories and wildlife books, described Furbish as an accomplished naturalist and the foremost authority on the New Brunswick woods. Neither Furbish nor Ganong, however, thought quite as highly of Long. In June 1907 Caspar Whitney, editor of *The Outdoor Magazine*, would write to Ganong wondering how Long could have seen so much New Brunswick wildlife and in such intimate detail after only a few occasional visits. Whitney suspected "fairy tales" and was pleased to have his intuition confirmed by Ganong who disapproved of Long's anthropomorphizing of animals. One suspected invention was Long's description of hawks at the head of the Tobique spearing fish

Mauran I. Furbish on Visitors Island, c. 1902. NEW BRUNSWICK MUSEUM, GANONG COLLECTION: 1987-17-1218-212

and dropping them into the water for their young to practice diving for food. The story seems to have been based on Furbish's description of a wounded gaspereau floating on a lake. Recognizing the Tobique setting from Long's description, Furbish, on seeing a loon not too distant from their canoe called out: "Eh, Mr. Loon, how about that story Mr. Long told about spearing the fish?" The loon answered immediately with its weird laugh: "Ha, ha, ha."

In a letter written in 1910 to Manly Hardy, Fannie Eckstorm's father, Ganong expressed delight that Hardy had been cited favourably in Ernest Thompson Seton's recent book on mammals and that Long was conspicuous by his absence. American president Theodore Roosevelt was even more direct than Seton, recommending, according to Ganong's sister Susan, that Long's books be removed from school libraries. William T. Hornaday, director of the New York Zoological Park, in response to Ganong's NHSNB article on animal romancers in 1905, characterized Long's combination of plausibility and lack of scruple as a public hazard. In his *Bulletin* article, Ganong also dismissed the popular animal stories of New Brunswick's Charles Goodridge Roberts, Bliss Carman's cousin. While Roberts inferred (rather than claimed) his animal stories were based on experience rather than, as Ganong suggested, searches in libraries and museums, Ganong thought his ambivalence was enough to mislead his readers. In an unpublished manuscript on New Brunswick scenery, Ganong noted that Roberts's writings were usually "untramelled [*sic*] by too close attention to fact." The result of this and similar deceptions was that engaging works of fiction masqueraded as natural history. After reading Ganong's animal romancers article, W. H. Venning, a New Brunswicker who had spent a lifetime in the company of lumbermen, hunters, and fur buyers, hoped Ganong had managed to escape the bands of ferocious wolves that C. D. G. Roberts assured them still infested the woods of New Brunswick. According to Venning, no wolf had been spotted in New Brunswick for forty years.

In 1902 Ganong and Furbish embarked on another marathon: a two-stage, six-week venture to Serpentine Lake and the Graham Plains in the north central highlands. They went down the fifty-kilometre-long Serpentine River—the stream running like a racehorse—to the Tobique, poled up the Little Tobique, crossed to the Nepisiguit and then the Upsalquitch, descending the latter to the Restigouche and Campbellton. In the Adder Lake basin, which no physiographer or naturalist had ever visited, they spent two weeks surveying, mapping, and measuring distances with a simple homemade device, and sounding depths in the lakes. They climbed to the summit of Mount Carleton where they spent two hours photographing and taking angles. Ganong named two of the lakes Mauran and Whitney (the latter after Furbish's wife) and another Murray, his first wife's family name. Although rocky and thinly treed, the basin was alive with big game such as moose, caribou, and beaver. Moose in particular were abundant, and game trails were more evident than anywhere else he had been in New Brunswick. He considered the open Graham Plains to be the best caribou grounds in the province, and because they were not easily accessible they would make an ideal game refuge of the sort then being established in the States.

As a professional map-maker and skilled outdoorsman, Furbish brought out the best in Ganong, inspiring hymns to the wilderness and periodic professions of well-being. "Altogether a great day," Ganong wrote on the 1901 Tuadook trip, "the work included. It is a great joy with abounding strength to stride along these beautiful paths lightly... the heaviest loads, every pulse alive with strength and purest pleasure, or as one starts back for another load in the joy of health and full sympathy with the woods." He was almost as elated at the end of the demanding and hazardous descent of the Little Southwest Miramichi: "We reached this place about 6 after a hard day. But all is serene so far as we are concerned, and it may rain as hard as it may please tonight if it will but give us a fair day tomorrow."

Mauran Furbish kept no travel journal—at least, not one that has survived—while G. U. Hay took notes and wrote them up as articles for the *Bulletin*. The only daily journals comparable to Ganong's were those of Arthur Henry Pierce. Pierce was a professor of psychology at Smith, interested in wildlife, game in particular, and photography. The Eastman Kodak hand-held, roll-film, folding cameras Pierce and Ganong carried on their expeditions came on the market in the 1890s. Unlike the earlier coated glass plates, dry roll film was light and portable; it could be changed without access to a darkroom, stored, and developed later. Pierce also relished the outdoor life and understood the need to chart the wilderness, but not above everything else. Ganong may have been a thoughtful and genial companion, but he was also so single-minded that he never lost sight of his prime objectives of measuring, mapping, and recording. His later field journals are overwhelmingly matter-of-fact itineraries that describe the daily life of the camp, weather, travelling conditions, and the availability of trout—the only diversion he seems to have allowed himself—for the pot and for sport. In his journals Pierce was more inclined to digress, remarking on books that he might be reading, the work habits of his companion, or the pleasures of camp life: from the "companionable bubbling" of beans

Ganong atop Mt. Ganong, named for him by Mauran Furbish, 1901. NEW BRUNSWICK MUSEUM, GANONG COLLECTION: 1987-17-1218-194

in the pot to the " unearthly" sound of loons that surpassed anything he had ever heard in the realms of wild and varied sound. On reaching a settlement and receiving news, he would also comment occasionally on world affairs.

For Ganong in the New Brunswick woods there was no other world. In his personal and professional correspondence there are occasional references to the First World War but very few in his field journals. He told Fannie Eckstorm the most effective contribution he could make to the war effort was to keep civilization going, by (in summer) attending to "Indian matters" and to New Brunswick. On two occasions his reveries while canoeing in coastal waters were interrupted by the RCMP

Camp Smith College, 1903. New Brunswick Museum, Ganong Collection: 1987-17-1219-87

who needed reassurance he was not spying for the Germans. On the first occasion he averted suspicion by proving he knew far more about Saint John and New Brunswick than the officer. The second time, he had to demonstrate the box in his canoe contained scientific equipment, not a radio.

Pierce's first trip with Ganong was on the Tobique and the Miramichi in August 1903. They poled up the Little Tobique to Nictau Lake, crossed to the Nepisiguit, and descended it to the mouth of the wild and unnavigable South Branch of the Nepisiguit. After days of hauling the canoe upstream they set up a base camp on a tranquil section of the river. The two professors named it Paradise Pond in an affectionate nod to the Smith campus. They named the camp Seelye after the college's admired president. From Camp Seelye they tramped up the South Branch to the base of Big Bald Mountain, known in Mi'kmaw as Kagoot, in the heart of the north central highlands. From Bald Mountain Ganong took sightings of surrounding peaks, climbed several of them, and worked out their relationship to the headwaters of the Nepisiguit, Upsalquitch, and Miramichi river systems. They returned to their base camp on Paradise Pond and from there they hauled their canoe to the source of the Northwest Miramichi, a deadwater that it shared with the Nepisiguit. By late afternoon Pierce was so played out that they were forced to stop and camp. On the descent to Newcastle, a Mi'kmaq across the river was the first human they had seen for three weeks.

For Pierce, the trip was a baptism of ice. Below Bald Mountain it was so cold that Ganong talked amusingly of making a dash for the pole before setting out for the summit. In the central highlands, frosts on high ground hard enough to whiten the vegetation were frequent in late August. In their journal entries, both men wrote of socks freezing overnight in their boots and of ice on the water pail. Ganong also spoke of capturing the scalp of Bald Mountain, a fairly easy prey once they had warmed up. Covered only with reindeer moss and low bushes, the ground offered the most "magnificent semi-open tramping" that they had ever experienced. On their return to camp after a cold, wet day of tramping Pierce wrote: "Good supper—beans, flapjacks, cocoa and a strong and satisfied feeling of being at home. Beautiful clear night. Cold."

The following July (1904) on a trip to Gover Lake, Ganong and Pierce headed for the Graham Plains and the Tuadook lakes, "a very remote and interesting region" in the very heart of the New Brunswick highlands, as Ganong described it. Because of its remoteness the lake basin had been little visited, only scantily surveyed, seldom mentioned in print, and "wholly unstudied by scientific men." They then crossed from Tuadook

Arthur Henry Pierce portaging to the Northwest Miramichi. NEW BRUNSWICK MUSEUM, GANONG COLLECTION: 1987-17-1219-68

to Renous Lake and descended the Renous River to Blackville and the Southwest Miramichi to Newcastle; a trip spanning more than three weeks of July and August. At the beginning of the trip Ganong leapt into a brook with only a few centimetres of water and injured a tendon in his left calf. For more than twenty-four hours, he hobbled about the camp leaning on an axe or frying-pan handle, insisting Pierce eat a greater share of the food and do a minimum of camp work. To their great relief, the leg behaved "admirably" and Ganong was able to tramp again after a day or so of rest. They estimated distances by pacing, each taking a side on the smaller lakes. For accurate measurements of up to two kilometres they used a fifteen-metre tape, marking the intervals with toilet paper. Ganong mapped by triangulation, measuring a base line and taking angles to fixed points from each end. The distance of any points visible from the two ends, and of those points from one another, could be calculated by applying the mathematical relation between the angles and sides of a triangle. His tools were a compass and a telescopic alidade for measuring angles and a plane table for plotting or mapping. His other indispensable tool (or skill) was his ability to draw ground, to see how features were related and transfer these impressions to paper. Sketching makes the map, and it called for an artistic sense as well as long experience in the field.

The Gover Lake trip was Pierce's first experience of field mapping, and he was a little bemused by the behaviour. In lake basins that had never been mapped, or been mapped incorrectly, Ganong was always pacing and surveying. In the mornings before breakfast, Pierce remarked, Ganong was up his usual hill, taking sightings. After supper he often went out again. On a beautiful, breezy evening on the upper Graham Plain, designed for sedentary reflection, Pierce wrote: "G took some angles while I lay in the shade, watching the setting sun, taking a nap and smoking." On "loaf days," Sundays, while Pierce read and attended to camp chores—mending and darning—Ganong plotted his findings and "with his usual untiring physiographic interest" made short excursions on lake and land. Pierce was not so driven and, not sharing Ganong's wider interests, was sometimes puzzled and impatient with their apparent inconsequence. At Pokemouche the following summer he referred to his companion's "daffy business" as Ganong went off to examine some of the tidal inlets.

Pierce's journals chronicle the strength of Ganong's single-mindedness. One afternoon Ganong returned to camp jubilant at finding a sizeable stream crossing a portage road that had not been recorded on any sketch or map. On hearing this, Pierce ribbed him on the score of his obsession with exact facts—of the dimensions of potholes and the location and size of brooks—as if any of it signified. "But," he corrected himself later in his journal, "it does to him. A <u>complete</u> map is his only satisfaction—complete as far as legs and eyes can make it in the want of more instruments of precision." Unlike George Hay and Ganong, Pierce did not delight in portages that required moving in three stages and, when plagued by thoughts of "home sweet home" on wet days, he took solace in the sailor's maxim from Frank C. Bullen's *Cruise of the Cachelot:* "It's dogged as does it." On the *Cachelot,* doggedness brought the whale back to the ship. Ganong, on the other hand, needed no energizing maxims: "He is utterly tireless," noted Pierce, "and tramps and surveys all the time."

Although Pierce occasionally was so exhausted he had to request a stop, Ganong was generally considerate and always celebrated Pierce's July 30 birthday by declaring a day of rest. The morning, Pierce noted on his 1904 birthday on their Gover Lake trip, was like a Sunday; they spent it loafing and puttering around the tent. Later in the day they had a big birthday dinner of soup, hardtack, sweet chocolate, nuts, oats, raisins, and tea followed by a paddle on the lake. "Ganong [insisted] that I be the passenger though I paddled most of the way," Pierce wrote, bemused. To end the day, they sat around a cheerful fire supping a brown sugar birthday toddy. "It was a capital way to pass a birthday & G did everything possible to make the day a notable one for me."

The rest of the trip down to the Miramichi and Newcastle, however, was hard going and at times, for Pierce, lonely. He found hauling a loaded canoe in shallow rock-strewn water "tough work, worse even than the [despised] tramping." In Ganong's notebooks there are very few references to hardship. On the Renous, heading toward the Southwest Miramichi and hoping for easier passage, an inspector of hunting and fishing camps assured them they would have no trouble. As they approached the southwest branch, however, they encountered a stretch of water even more daunting than the Nepisiguit. "The P.M.," Pierce noted, "started in with boulders,

Ye mightie trippe of ye yeare A.D. 1904

W.F.G. brings	Each brings	A.H.P. brings
Provisions (List A)	blanket	Tent
Bags etc for do.	pet fly-bane	Cooking outfit (except articles
Portage harnesses	rubber coat	specified under B.)
Canoe + poles + paddles	note books	1 heavy axe
Surveying outfit	compass	photographic outfit
Maps	towel + soap	field glasses
{1 light axe + guard	camp-shoes	ballast – 1 qt
B {fry-pan	extra shirt &	Provisions List BB
{knives, forks, spoons	trousers	stone for axes
fishing outfit	cotton bag for clothes	axe guard
dunnage (clothes) bag	big knife	rope
catch-all canvas bag.	match box	Cans for coffee
Stock of matches	fly nets	
2 anewids	bile clefs	Rucksack
thermometer + max & min.	tooth brush	α
Small medicine-outfit		
white lead + rosin for canoe canvas	tablet note	
nails, wire, string etc. bit nails		
2 bars soap	2 hot water bags	
cooking stove		
dish rags	Post cards	
Needles thread etc.	Fork bag –	
Rope	note note tablets –	
wax ends + awl	tape measure	
Candles		
tool-knife		

Provisions – List A

Hardtack	20 lbs	25 ?
Sugar	35 "	
Ham	30 "	
Beans	20 "	
Pork	15 "	
Rice	12 " 8 lb	
Raisins		
B.wheat flour	} 6 pkg.	
(Done up in oil-skin)		
Corn meal	3 lbs	
apples	4 "	
Tea	1 lb	
Coffee	2 lbs	
Salt	req	
Butter	10 lb	
Molasses	8 qts	
pepper		

Thumb tacks

coffee pot ?

Provisions – List BB
10 army rations (3 hav 1/2)
2 lbs cocoa
1/2 doz soup tablets

bottle malted milk
2 lbs nut kernels

Ganong's gear and provision list, 1904. NEW BRUNSWICK MUSEUM, GANONG COLLECTION:
F454-14

Valuable —
Please return to
me W.F.G.

Proposals for ye walking trippe — 1905   W.F.G - A.H.P

Plan — go provisioned for 2 wks — and extend trip beyond
that in proportion to fish we get - extreme limit 3 wks.

Motto — cut down every ounce of weight

W.F.G. brings
- The maps
- Small anerord
- Max + min therm.
- ✓ Compass
- ✓ light axe
- ✓ tent & floor
- ✓ frying pan
- ✓ 2 spoons my 2 R plates
- ✓ 2 forks
- ✓ 2 portage harness
- ✓ stock of matches
- ✓ wax ends + awl
- ✓ fishing lines + flies
- ✓ lint + court plaster
- ✓ provisions in bags
- ✓ general carrying bags (2)
- ✓ fragment of soap (didn't take)

Each brings
- note book
- 1 pkg. fly-bane
- knife
- ✓ blanket
- light rubber coat
- camp moccasins
- ✓ match box
- fly nets
- my socks
- Ginger (for tooth ache) —

A. H. P. brings
- ✓ Camera with 3 doz. films
- tent (with floor)
- ✓ small kettle
- ✓ coffee pot (or smaller tin)
- ✓ cups 3 nested   smaller kettle?
- ✓ stone for axe
- ✓ some string
- — 2 coats —

For clothes I purpose to take only my shirt trousers
socks & boots I have on, + 1 shirt & 1 pair
woollen drawers, which will do to put on if I
get wet — no others except 1 extra pair socks.

Provisions.

army rations	8		Coffee	½ lb	
Hardtack	4		cocoa	½ lb	
Rice	5				
Pork	4		salt —		
Sugar	12		apples	1 lb	
			nut kernels nuts —	1 lb	
Butter	3 lbs		weight with bags		
Raisins	2 lbs		about		
Buckwheat	2 pkgs		50	lbs	
Corn meal	½ lb				
tea	¼ lb				
Ham	5 lbs				

I think our
packs at the
start will come
within 40
lbs each my
Easily

— Provisions were
abundant — had some
over — got fair no of
fish — none too many

Ganong's gear and provision list, 1905. New Brunswick Museum, Ganong Collection:
F454-16

then more boulders and bigger boulders, strewn in the most fiendish and diabolical intricacy that the malevolent one himself could devise. It was tug and pull and lift and squirm, all the while slipping and sliding, wrenching the entire body and making one wonder what the object of it all was anyway." They moved their gear in stages of about a quarter of a mile then carried the upturned canoe on their shoulders stepping "with infinite care" from boulder to boulder." Ganong concluded that the Renous was rougher than any river of similar size and drop in the province. The forty-nine-day trip ended at Newcastle with Pierce swearing, after the Renous trials, he would never do this sort of thing again.

July 8, 1905, however, found Pierce, his distress forgotten, with Ganong about to venture into "Darkest New Brunswick": the northern highlands. To map and do as much physiographic work as possible in the remote terrain, Ganong had planned a complex foot or packing trip via the Tobique to Gover Lake, Big Bald Mountain, and the source of the Sevogle. They would then descend the Sevogle to the Northwest Miramichi, ascend it, and go down the Nepisiguit to Bathurst. They reached Bathurst on July 29 where, on the eve of Pierce's birthday, they saw a variety/vaudeville show at the opera house. After a short rest, and supplied with a canoe, they made their way to the headwaters of the Tracadie River and canoed down it to its mouth. From there they paddled and sailed the canoe via the shore lagoons to Miscou Island, returning along the north shore to Caraquet. On the packing trip they followed portage and animal paths (often one and the same) as well as lumber roads or trails and slept in unoccupied lumber camps whenever these were available. As always, Ganong frequently stopped to make sightings wherever there was an elevation.

Their packing trip the following year from Newcastle to Gaugas and Frieze Lakes in Northumberland County was Pierce's least satisfying excursion. The July weather was alternately wet, or hot and humid, and the flies ferocious. They got off to a bad start. After "a horrible night" during the first week—the mosquitoes were relentless—Pierce woke before first light, noting Ganong had gone gallivanting upstream to record and take sightings. "I am to pack up." After twelve days of difficult tramping through rough, isolated country after leaving Gaugus Lake they reached Frieze Lake.

Ganong exulted at having reached the most inaccessible lake in New Brunswick. "But what a lake!" Pierce later noted sarcastically. "A low, boggy [mass] of water from innumerable springs, oozing out of warmish water." Tired, his heart "jumping" after an exhausting day, Pierce described it as a wretched part of the country, and declared the sooner they were out of it the better. In some places, the going was so difficult the pair's progress was reduced to a kilometre and a half per hour. Longing for comfort and society by the end of the trip, Pierce wrote: "Off at last for civilization. Heaven be praised." On the last day Ganong asked him if he would do the chores—wash up and clean the food bags—while he surveyed in preparation

W. F. Ganong and A. H. Pierce near the source of the Northwest Miramichi, July 1908.
New Brunswick Museum, Ganong Collection: 1987-17-1223-95

for an imminent trip with his brother. Pierce consented "complacently," but noted that much of what he did was of the wage-earning variety. "Don't do it again!" he advised himself. "And don't forget this time!...Remember also that hardship without adequate reward is foolishness."

Predictably, Pierce did forget. Unable to resist invitations from Ganong, he accompanied him on three more trips: 1908, 1910, and 1912.

The 1908 trip was another sortie to the headwaters of the Southwest Miramichi in an attempt to solve the riddle of the two Miramichis: a turbulent, constricted river in the rough country above Boiestown, and a quieter less confined river in the more open and settled country below. They concentrated on physiography, exploring the headwaters of the Miramichi and neighbouring streams and at the same time taking temperature and barometric readings. It was a demanding trip. Ganong's single-mindedness continued to irritate Pierce, as did his habit of making frequent solitary excursions away from camp. On one of their rest days Pierce remained at the camp studying a photography manual while Ganong left for a twelve-kilometre trek to check the location of a lake; he failed to find it but comforted himself that he had acquired valuable physiographic knowledge. In his diary Pierce admitted to a need for greater companionship. Tired of their limited diet of trout and hardtack, he also admitted to a longing for fresh meat, fresh vegetables, and sweet desserts. Ganong, on the other hand, never complained.

On one of Ganong's brief absences from camp Pierce met five men, presumably Quebecois but speaking a patois he could barely follow, whom he understood to have travelled from Montreal via Saint John on their way to Plaster Rock. They were seeking work on the transcontinental railway. They had been three days in bush where they had expected to find fields and farms. On his return, Ganong confirmed Pierce's interpretation. Their own supplies were short, however, and they were unable to invite the five men to stay.

Toward the end of the trip Pierce, whose heartbeat was irregular, announced defeat, begging off a proposed trip to the Dungarvon. Unperturbed, Ganong thought he could get his brother to replace Pierce. "I shall be glad to be out," wrote Pierce. "A hard packing trip under the shadow of another's unshared interest is no longer the thing for me. I must not do it again. I have said this before but now I think it is driven in so that it will stick in memory." With his heart "running badly," and counting the days to Boiestown, he needed rest and diversion. Late one afternoon they sighted a camp on the opposite side of the river with smoke coming from its chimney. Pierce wanted to stop but Ganong insisted on pressing on, a lapse that left Pierce feeling "mildly wrathy." Hours later his wrath, disarmed by Ganong's perennial good nature, evaporated.

Two years later, so too had Pierce's resolution. In early August 1910 he found himself with Ganong on the Dungarvon River and lakes. They left Fredericton for Boiestown on the evening express for a three-to-four-week trip. They stayed at Boiestown overnight and portaged the next day to a lumber camp within a kilometre of the Dungarvon. When they asked the camp watcher, Mr. McDonald, if he was not lonely he replied, "No, he saw somebody about every week." Ganong found him a profane old fellow, but he made them a supper of biscuits and boiled corn, peas, and tomatoes. After a few days on the river they left their canoe in bushes (with a note explaining the circumstances) and a bag of provisions in an old lumber camp. They then embarked on a ten-day tramp. At Burton Lake they slept in an unoccupied sporting camp (Pringles) and borrowed the camp canoe to explore the lake. After a splendid sleep in camp bunks they packed for a three-day trip to the Louis Lake group. Ganong had long wanted to see Louis Lake and it did not disappoint—clear water, rocky shores, fine wooded ridges, and so full of loons he wanted to spend the night just to hear them. On the lake they found a well-built lean-to in a pretty place and if not the hoped-for canoe then a serviceable raft of hewn logs with two poles, enabling them to circumnavigate the lake.

On that trip Pierce photographed, read, examined beaver dams, and ate "delicious" blueberries while Ganong walked, took angles, and sketched. Pierce had brought a copy of Mark Twain's *Tramp Abroad*. Where there were no lumber or portage roads they navigated by compass, particularly over burnt ground where paths had been obliterated. By mid-August their supplies were getting low and they had to get back to their stored provisions. On their return to the Dungarvon, McDonald put them up at the depot camp and fed them potatoes, boiled salt trout, biscuits, and tea, Ganong pumping him all the while with questions about the Dungarvon and adjacent country. To complete a trip that, for Pierce, had felt almost like a holiday, they made their way down to the Southwest Miramichi, negotiating rough and boulder-strewn patches before reaching Beaubears Island on August 25.

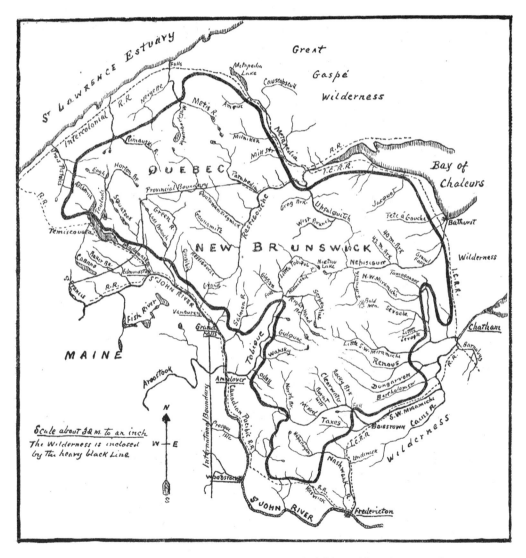

Ganong's map of the north-central highlands; J. W. Bailey's "Great New Brunswick Wilderness." NEW BRUNSWICK MUSEUM, GANONG COLLECTION: NHS-V24-404

Pierce's final trip with Ganong was to Green River, Madawaska County, in August 1912. Ganong pronounced it well nigh ideal in results and pleasure. The objective was to study the physiography and enjoy fishing. The men met at Woodstock en route to Edmundston immediately following a trip Ganong had made with his brother Walter in Queens and Westmorland counties. They portaged to the headwaters of Green River, a tributary of the St. John, through days of heavy rain. For the last leg of the portage, they exchanged their wagon for a drag sled or "jumper" that allowed them to negotiate windfalls and other obstacles in the road. The rain persisted yet they remained cheerful and, drawing upon their long experience in the woods, relatively comfortable. It was the coldest and wettest of all their trips.

Movement on the water was also difficult. To travel upstream, they poled and dragged the canoe with a special haul Ganong had attached to the bow. Near the end of the ascent Pierce recorded that Ganong rejected an opportunity to see the uppermost (the fifth and sixth) in the chain of lakes in the Green River system on grounds that he had already seen the surrounding country and did not need to see the lakes themselves. Pierce, however, was not convinced. The lakes were in Quebec, and Quebec, as Pierce intimated in his notes, was not Ganong's country.

Despite the exceptionally cold, wet weather, Pierce enjoyed the trip. He found the country particularly attractive and the poor weather, Ganong's preoccupations forgiven, had not affected the customary geniality of camp life. It would be his last excursion with Ganong. Two years later, Ganong's "devoted companion," as he described Pierce on their Sevogle trip, died in Northampton from a short—and, for the Smith community, shocking—illness that began as a cold and developed rapidly into pleurisy and fatal pneumonia. Pierce Hall, the psychology building at Smith, is named for him.

Chapter 8

LATER JOURNEYS

Ganong's canoe and packing trips continued, sometimes with a companion and sometimes without. When alone he took a small, lightweight tent of his own design, and a three-and-a-half-metre canvas canoe, both of which he could carry himself. In 1916 he ran the rapids on the last nineteen kilometres of Eel River—which the First Nations always portaged around—and wrote to Fannie Eckstorm about "that most glorious feeling of rapid running." He also told her one of his great outdoor pleasures was listening to rain hammering on canvas: "I enjoy tremendously the sound of pouring rain especially if hard driven by wind…in a tight tent, nestled down in warm, dry blankets. This is the triumph of winning the battle of wits against nature, I suppose."

On his accompanied trips his companions were his brothers, Walter and Arthur; his friends William Laskey and A. R. MacDonald, both from Fredericton; and Leonard Smith from Grangeville, who was a particular favourite. On a number of occasions Ganong chose Aboriginal companions. In 1912 he went with the canoe builder Lewey (Louis) Francis down the Letang and among the Passamaquoddy islands to Cobscook Bay and back by canoe. That same summer he and Noel Lewey canoed through the Schoodic lakes in Maine and down the St. Croix to Milltown. The objectives were Aboriginal lore and, above all, names of places and features that had never been recorded. In a letter to Fannie Eckstorm he wrote that names and lore that existed only in the minds of living First Nations were rapidly vanishing and must be saved promptly if at all.

In the summer of 1916 Ganong spent ten days among the Passamaquoddy in the bay and the St. Croix region, five of them alone in a canoe, and "rescued a rich and wholly unrecorded nomenclature, much of it charming" that yielded not only new names but shed new light on their construction. He thought there were four to six times as many place names in Passamaquoddy waters as yet unrecorded, some of them embodying legends of great interest. Later, he went on foot with Lewey Francis's son, Anthony, to Long Lake and Ormond Lake, then down New River to its mouth.

In 1922 he accompanied John Nicholas, a renowned guide and hunter whom he regarded as one of the best informed of the Passamaquoddy, around the Passamaquoddy islands. Ganong slept in his small tent and Nicholas made a nest with furs, blankets, and a tarpaulin beneath the overturned canoe. Foghorns disturbed their sleep. Although pleasant company, John Nicholas was a disappointing informant and such a terrible cook that Ganong cooked for himself. By Ganong's reckoning, Nicholas must have been well over eighty, and his memory for details understandably failing. Having cruised, camped, and conversed with the most informed of the living Aboriginals, Ganong concluded Nicholas had now exhausted the stock of surviving lore.

None of Ganong's later companions kept a journal, and the format of his own daily journals never changed. On most journeys he tried to cover new ground, but on others he reworked ground previously covered, "for the exact study of details." His most unusual solo tour was a three-week bicycle tour in August 1908 through the backcountry of Charlotte, Carleton, Victoria, and York Counties following his exploration of the headwaters of the Southwest Miramichi with Arthur Pierce. Lightweight with a high gear and no brakes or coasters, Ganong's bike was "practically a racer." Fitted to the frame was a valise that held clothing, a compass, and simple mapping and cooking equipment. As a substitute for a postponed and much rougher trip in the Dungarvon woods he said he felt like a man he once heard of who left America expecting to hunt big game in Africa but who ended by making a tour of English cathedral towns. Ganong left St. Stephen on August 6 and stayed in hotels and boarding houses. His route was through Vanceboro and Forest City in Maine to Grand Lake, and then back and forth through Carleton and Victoria Counties and parts of Maine to Andover and Perth. He described it as a glorious journey replete with pleasure and profit, both physical and physiographic.

In 1913 he covered old ground on a twelve-day trip alone down the Magaguadavic River and lakes to St. George, a river system he'd traversed several years earlier but wished to revisit. In the interim he edited the journals of the surveyors who had mapped the river in 1796–97 and wanted, as he put it, to "travel in their company." Aside from the physiography,

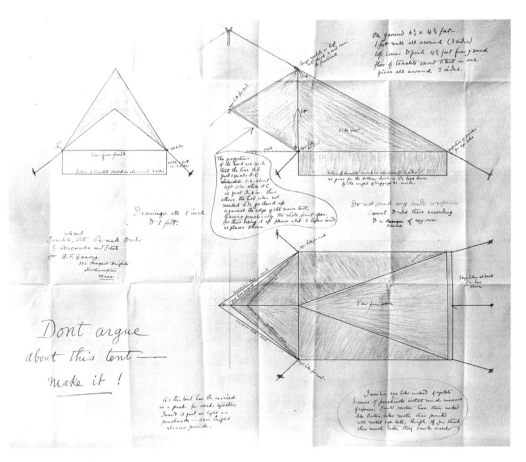

Ganong's peremptory instructions for making a custom-made tent. New Brunswick Museum, Ganong Collection: 1987-17-1347

Ganong was interested in the characteristics of the places to which they had applied Aboriginal names. On that trip he hoped to find canoe-maker Lewey Francis at home, using a broken axe handle as an excuse for a Sunday visit. Francis was not at home and although his clock was still ticking, indicating he must be nearby, Ganong could not linger. Later solo trips by canoe were on the Oromocto, the St. John, and the Kennebecasis. He used the railways to get his canoe to the starting points, and for propulsion on the wider, open stretches of the rivers, a hand-made sail.

In July 1914 he left Rothesay for a much-anticipated solo trip to study the falls of the Pollet River. He drove to the head of the Kennebecasis and went down the Pollet River by canoe, mapped the falls and rapids, and when advised not to take his canoe through a section of the rapids beneath wire fences that crossed the river, he hired "a good little horse" for the day. He then canoed down the Petitcodiac to the head of tide then poled back up it, and via tributary streams returned to the upper Kennebecasis and made his way down to Hampton and Rothesay. The ten-day excursion had given him "a much better grasp of the construction of the country."

Five days later Ganong embarked on an eighteen-day packing or walking trip with Leonard Smith of Grangeville. They carried their own outfit and provisions. From the lower Nepisiguit, near Bathurst, they crossed the rugged northern highlands to Tuadook Lake on the headwaters of the Southwest Miramichi, then made their way south to Boiestown. The trip brought the first intimations of frailty; in his notes, Ganong allowed that a long packing trip might be too hard for a person in his fifty-first year and that in wild New Brunswick the consequences of breaking a bone could be serious. The following summer, however, (1915) the risks of injury had apparently been shelved and Ganong's valour restored. He was off alone again. He left Rothesay for McAdam for a two-week trip canoeing on the Upper Shogomic, descended it to the St. John, was portaged to Harvey, and then went down the Digdeguash to Passamaquoddy. His aim was to check miscellaneous physiographic and archeological data. At McAdam he met the Saint John naturalist and entomologist William MacIntosh, curator of the NHSNB Museum from 1898 to 1932 and the first director of the New Brunswick Museum. MacIntosh was to take a party down the St. John from Woodstock, and on meeting him Ganong weakened momentarily, writing in his notebook: "My, I wish I could take a trip like that." But he recovered quickly. From McAdam he took a train that dropped his canoe and baggage on a path leading to the nearby Shogomic lakes. Watching the train and the civilization it represented disappearing down the line was, he recorded, "a supremely happy moment." He changed into his "fighting togs" and began hauling his gear down to the lake. Later that summer, in August 1915, he and Leonard Smith embarked on another packing trip to the upper Tetagouche River and lakes, crossed to the Jacquet River, and tramped down its fine length to the coast.

Ganong's objectives on these canoe and packing trips were primarily scientific, but not exclusively so. He spelled out his creed, in a Prospero-like summing-up, in the endnotes of a manuscript on the physiography of the province written in the 1920s:

The scientific and historical results, however, have not been the only reward, and perhaps not the chief incentive to these journeys, even though I have felt therein the joy of the primitive hunter, and bringing back the spoils to book. For there has been the profound satisfaction in the successful accomplishment of difficult physical feats, when, with only a chosen companion, without aid from guide or other helpers, we found our own way across uncharted wilderness, transported our own outfit through wide forests, worked our own canoe along rivers foaming with rapids, and kept ourselves safe and comfortable against all the odds and hazards of the woods. Then there has been the great charm, known to all explorers, in being the first to behold with seeing eyes so many remote places, and in making and recording the observations and surveys, crude though they are, which brought some part of the world into the light of exact knowledge. More potent still has been the attraction of the primitive life free from the trammels, galling though essential, of civilized life: the pulsing health that makes one feel like a new-made beastie…and above all in the joy of those moments of elation when nature and self vibrate together in complete harmony.

Elsewhere, in a manuscript account of New Brunswick scenery, Ganong described the thrilling sensation of perfect attunement with his surroundings as a "cosmic emotion." Age, however, would weaken both his pulsing health and his relish of the primitive life. In 1920 he had a camper top, equipped with a bed and lockers, built onto the body of a Ford chassis. It was a method of travel he'd considered and worked on for some time. On test trips the camper part worked well, the vehicle less so. His first journey was to Fredericton via the Gagetown road. He called it vagabonding. In 1921, he told Fannie Eckstorm he was going to spend the summer "cruising about the province, filling in gaps, chumming with Indians, lumbermen, guides, fishermen and other really interesting people." That July he took the "Gypsy Ford" north from Rothesay to Grand Falls, Fort Francis, and Temiscouta and then back down the St. John to Houlton and Woodstock. South of Woodstock he and his companions found Monument Road leading to the U.S. boundary line. They left the car on the Canadian side and, after walking through a field, found the monument Ganong had so long wanted to see. The cut stones were lying in the grass near the original post, which was much decayed but with lettering still decipherable. They followed the course of Monument Brook, as the 1797 surveyors must have done.

In 1923, Ganong passed another marker: he remarried at age fifty-nine. His first wife, Jean Murray (Muriel) Carman, had died in 1920. They had no children. Anna Hobbet, Ganong's second wife, was the daughter of Norwegians and grew up on a farm in Eagle Grove, Iowa. She was a graduate of the University of Iowa and an instructor in geology at Smith. The couple had two children: William Francis, born in July 1924, and Ann, born in September 1925. Ganong delighted in them, but he confided to his friend Prowse that their relatively late arrival in his life (he was now in his sixties) imposed on him the duties of a father when his instincts were those of a grandfather. In the summer of 1923, just before the birth of their son, Ganong and Anna camped in the upper reaches of the Kennebecasis east of Sussex where Anna studied moraines and Ganong surveyed. September of 1923 found them at the camp of a friend near St. Andrews where, to celebrate his recent marriage, Ganong wrote his field notes in Old English: "Ye true and faithfulle William F. Ganong and Ann, hys true and lovinge Wyffe, the same being two scientifical Johnnies, more fain to prye into ye private affaires of ye Dame Nature than to ete the brede of Lyffe though not averse to ye latter on occasion, the more if accompanyed by some pye."

The week-long trip at the beginning of September might have been a honeymoon, but it didn't interrupt their prying into the affairs of Dame Nature, "ye Manne makinge studies of ye topographie, and ye Ladye on ye rocks, being learned in them and their interesting wayes." On the fourth day they climbed Chamcook Mountain near St. Andrews from whose summit the "glorious view" across Passamaquoddy Bay to Deer Island, Maine, made "ye scientifical couple love ye country much, and also yielded facts of consequence about ye physiographie." In general, how-ever, they did not spare the Ford, driving to the top of ridges and des-cending "like ye verie helle...to ye distresse of the Forde which did make proteste by sundry motley noyses and many jumpes in ye manner of ye bucking horses. But we did finde out maney factes, and had one grande

Ganong's Ford Model T, modified to accommodate a camper bed and cupboards, 1920.
New Brunswick Museum, Ganong Collection: 1987-17-1225-31

and gloriouss tyme." On leaving the "wylde and lonely places for the busie hauntes of Manne," they would take the train for Chicago and Iowa to make "ye acquaintance of ye newe mother in lawe."

Children prevented further joint field trips, but Ganong's solo canoe trips and motor trips continued. According to Anna, he would be gone for days and even weeks at a time. In the late 1920s he made several motor trips and found himself tinkering with engines, not canoes and paddles. He seemed familiar with the general mechanics but needed help when the vehicle wouldn't start. The longest trips were with the photographer H. W. Beecher Smith of Sussex. In 1927 he and Beecher Smith drove to the Chignecto region in a Buick coupe, where they had to be hauled out of a ditch, and July of the following year they took the same vehicle, fully fitted for comfort, for a ten-day "observation[al], impressionistic and photographic trip" around the "Northern Circle." They drove first to Moncton, Shediac, Buctouche, and Chatham, and then along the North Shore to Bathurst, Campbellton, and Dalhousie. At Dalhousie, Beecher Smith photographed in the evening light, and at Campbellton they loafed

Ganong and his second wife, Anna Hobbet, camping, 1923. New Brunswick Museum, Ganong Collection: 1987-17-648-2

around for a day waiting for the rainy, murky weather to clear enough for photographs. From Campbellton they went up the Restigouche to Matapedia and then along the St. Lawrence to Rivière du Loup. To complete the circle they came down the St. John to Edmundston and Grand Falls, photographing all the way, and then finally to Hartland and Fredericton and across to Rothesay and Sussex. It was a "fine trip of 850 miles without the slightest car trouble."

In 1929, again with Beecher Smith and the Buick, Ganong made two short circular journeys in southwest New Brunswick. First from St. Stephen, where they met, along the coast to Maces Bay, New River, Blacks Harbour, Beaver Harbour, the east side of Lake Utopia to Saint George, and then back to St. Stephen via Chamcook and St. Andrews. Then, after an interval, north from St. Stephen to Rolling Dam, Fredericton, and the federal Experimental Farm, and then downriver to Gagetown where on the night of a great storm they camped cozily and comfortably in the lee of the lighthouse. Finally home: Sussex for Smith, Rothesay for Ganong. Ganong described it as "a most successful and pleasant trip." It was his last entry in a bulging collection of manuscript notebooks.

Chapter 9

~~~~~~~~~~~~~~~~~~~~~

THE FIRST NATIONS
AND THE FRENCH

O f the inhabitants of New Brunswick, two groups in particular
interested Ganong: the First Nations and the French. He had
a working knowledge of both the Maliseet and Mi'kmaw languages, and for decades he was the leading English scholar of the Acadian
period. He published a map of Aboriginal routes of travel in 1895, and
in 1889 he wrote the introduction to Montague Chamberlain's *Maliseet
Vocabulary*, published by the Harvard Cooperative Society. Chamberlain
was from Saint John, and before moving to Harvard to become assistant
secretary of the Harvard Corporation and secretary of the Lawrence Scientific School, he had been a vice-president of the Natural History Society.

Ganong's 1899 monograph on historic sites for *Transactions* begins
with a survey of the Aboriginal period. He described the geographical
distribution of both tribes, the sites of their villages, camping places, and
burial grounds, and explained the manner and the routes of their travel. It
was another first attempt at a comprehensive treatment of a subject that
previous historians may have approached but not engaged.

As had earlier travellers and chroniclers, Ganong identified two distinct
tribes, the Mi'kmaq and Maliseet, and assigned to them territories based upon
the use and occupancy of river basins. The Mi'kmaq controlled the northern

and eastern areas, including the basin of the Miramichi and the head of the Bay of Fundy and the Maliseet controlled the St. John and its tributaries as well as the Passamaquoddy region. With the Maliseet occupying the Kennebecasis and Canaan River basins and the Mi'kmaq the Petitcodiac, the traditional dividing line would probably have been in the region of Sussex. The Passamaquoddy were a geographical division of the Maliseet as were the Penobscot in Maine. All were Algonquin and spoke related dialects.

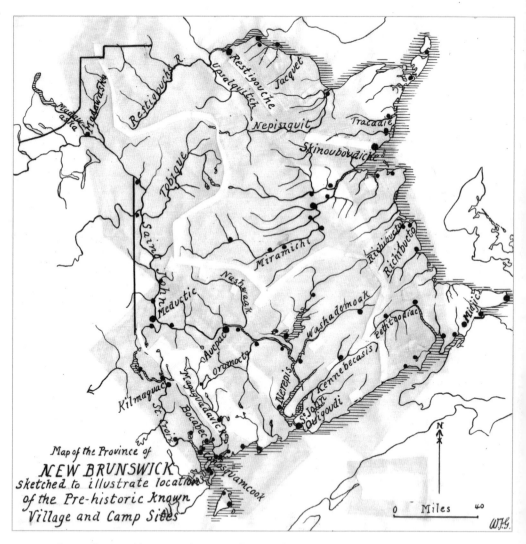

Ganong's map of known prehistoric villages and campsites. NEW BRUNSWICK MUSEUM, GANONG COLLECTION: F448-32

To this primary division Ganong added the rider, based mainly on the evidence of place names and French colonial era writings, that at the time of the first European contact the Mi'kmaq probably occupied the lower Saint John valley as far upstream as the head of tide near Fredericton. To demonstrate Mi'kmaw and Maliseet territories, Ganong drew a line on a small-scale map (twenty-five kilometres to the centimetre) known subsequently as the "Ganong line." Modern ethnographers and historians question its accuracy, especially in the region of the lower Saint John, and Ganong himself modified some of his earlier views, but it is the division still adopted by makers of standard atlases and by the province and the courts in matters of tribal hunting rights.

For his survey of camping, village sites, and burial grounds Ganong divided the province into river basins—in effect the band and tribal territories—and for each of the sixty-six sites identified he listed the attributes, often in great detail. He drew upon verbal sources, cartographic and documentary evidence, and his own observations, combining these with what he knew of Mi'kmaq and Maliseet ways of life. The largest villages occurred where favourable conditions came together: where fish, game, and spring water were readily available, where land was flat for wigwams and cultivation, and where portage routes were at hand. Burnt Church, the largest of the Aboriginal villages, occupied an elevated site at the junction of important coast and land routes. Its distinctive name refers to the breakup of the Acadian community by the English in 1758, and the burning to the ground of their stone church.

For hunting, war, and treaty making, the First Nations moved periodically through their own territories and those of neighbouring tribes. In historic times, the Mi'kmaq and Maliseet had never been at war, but the Mohawk were their perennial enemies. In New Brunswick, as Ganong noted repeatedly, the First Nations had a river system whose comprehensive coverage could not be equalled by any other province or state. Moreover, most of the rivers were navigable by canoe, the most versatile of vessels. One of the largest of them, the Maliseet four-person canoe, drew only four inches of water when partly loaded and, since it weighed less than a hundred pounds, could be overturned and carried over portage paths between the headwaters, the cross-struts resting on the shoulders

of the carriers. Due to the interlocking nature of the headwaters the portages generally were only a few miles long. Unlike the Aboriginals of
Massachusetts, which was less endowed with waterways, the Mi'kmaq
and the Maliseet were spared long treks through the woods. With a light,
three-metre pole, the canoe could also be forced up the swiftest of rivers
and be made to surmount rapids and low falls. If the water was too shallow
for the canoe to float, it could be shod with splints of cedar and dragged

The "Ganong Line" map, indicating Aboriginal territories. New Brunswick Museum,
Ganong Collection: F448-27

over wet stones. To the Maliseet and the Mi'kmaq of New Brunswick, the canoe was the equivalent of the pony to the First Nations of the west.

One of Ganong's objectives was to chart the exact courses of the portages before the physical evidence and memories were lost forever. Field research, interviews with both Aboriginal and European residents, and examination of old maps and texts enabled him, in his 1899 monograph, to identify more than forty portage routes linking the large rivers. Ganong illustrated the routes he'd traversed or surveyed with hand-drawn maps and augmented these with detailed notes. The Canaan–Petitcodiac portage, for example, "was a route much used in travel from the Beausejour (Cumberland) region to Quebec. The Washademoak, or Canaan River, is fairly easy of navigation to the portage. Since the North River, the continuation of the Petitcodiac, is not navigable, the portage path crossed from the Washademoak, about two miles above Nevers Brook, to the main Petitcodiac, which it reached about five miles below Petitcodiac Station. It was hence about twelve miles long, one of the longest of the important portages of the province."

TOPONYMY

In a 1911 issue of the *Transactions of the Royal Society*, Ganong published the first of a series of four articles on Maliseet and Mi'kmaw place names. He understood that names were keys, not only to language but also to culture. He dismissed his earlier, 1896 study, based mainly on hearsay, anecdote, and unexamined sources, as preliminary. The subsequent study he labelled "scientific." For a botanist, it was a remarkable exercise in etymology, the origins and meaning of words.

As with so much of his social and cultural history, Ganong's pursuit of Maliseet and Mi'kmaw names was driven by the need to record before the evidence vanished. He feared the then-current generation would be the last to retain anything of value to etymology or ethnology. Neither the Mi'kmaq nor the Maliseet had a written language or characters or symbols of any sort for reproducing words; the spoken languages had been corrupted by two hundred years of contact with Europeans. In general, young Aboriginals expressed no interest in the roots of their language, their customs, or their legends.

Fannie Hardy Eckstorm wrote that "modern Indian" was so different from "old Indian" as to be unintelligible even to her aged informants. Clara Neptune, Eckstorm's eighty-four-year-old chief informant, could not speak "old Indian," but she had a ninety-year-old cousin, Cecilia Barker, who could. "I fancy," said Neptune, "she is the last one who could do it." For many years living Aboriginals had given up trying to interpret unfamiliar words and constructions, dismissing the speakers with expressions like "She's old Indian; I don't know what she means." Lewey (Louis) Ketchum, one of Eckstorm's most valuable Aboriginal informants, complained that his grandchildren could not speak even the current version of his native tongue. Vocabulary, intonation, cadence, and rhythm had all changed. Among the Passamaquoddy and the Maliseet the very old were ridiculed for talking so "lazy," so slowly, and for the rhythmic, musical quality of their delivery. The young spoke more quickly, in shorter sentences—more in the matter-of-fact style of English.

Ganong specified three possible approaches to the study of Aboriginal place names: two well trodden and the third untried. In the conventional stage, recorders—often beguiled by the musicality and mystery of Aboriginal names—adopted the forms most pleasing to the imagination and the ear. Sanctioned by custom, these forms were adopted by popular guidebooks, tourist literature, and general historical works. There was not the slightest need of them meaning anything. Fannie Eckstorm described the American adoption of names as "something fearful and wonderful. They may come from anywhere and be tacked on anyhow." Ganong replied that Maritimers were lucky: Aboriginal names came mostly via the French, who researched them far more thoroughly than did English Americans. "The French," he added, "meant to get them right, but the English apparently made a stab at them, and then they stuck to the result and were satisfied, at least that seems true of the names that came to us.... So I don't wonder you have trouble with them."

Well-intentioned students of the languages were also culpable. Aboriginal nomenclature allowed the imagination so much scope that, as in history in general, there was always the inclination to make the facts fit the fancy, a hanging offence in Ganong's eyes. Other offences were more forgivable but no less damaging. Aboriginal informers, who had lost contact with older forms of the language, when asked to explain meanings would select roots that most resembled the modern form of the name, often with utterly misleading results. Philologists and missionaries made similar mistakes. Determined to identify origins, they ascribed meanings to roots quite unconnected to the modern words, leaving a subject more entangled with error than any other Ganong could think of.

As well as being mere sounds with their original meaning lost, Ganong found that Aboriginal names, whatever their provenance, were routinely shortened. He found also, to his surprise, that the pronunciations of uneducated country people were closer to the Aboriginal form than those of the educated who had fewer exchanges with either Maliseets or Mi'kmaqs. This seemed to disprove, in the case of names at least, that languages with a literature are more stable than those without.

The second stage of inquiry Ganong labelled "interrogational." The researcher collects all the available forms and interpretations of the names, and other information that bears on them, and attempts a collation. Any agreements demonstrated by the data were regarded as gospel. Most works on place nomenclature went only this far. At its best, the approach involved the retrieval of the earliest forms of the names from printed works, deeds, and other official documents, as well as data obtained by interviewing living Aboriginals. This was the stage reached in his earlier study.

The third stage, which had not been tried anywhere in Canada, Ganong called "investigational." It adopted the scientific method of induction. All preferences, preconceptions, and prejudices were expunged and all available sources of information examined and weighed carefully. Ancient deeds, grants, and maps were to be thoroughly rifled for the earliest (and least corrupted) recorded forms of the names, and notes made of all references in existing dictionaries, vocabularies, and grammars.

Ganong's chief living informant, Fannie Eckstorm, herself a Smith graduate (1888), was in some respects Ganong's Maine counterpart. She was the daughter of Manly Hardy, a fur trader and naturalist whom she sometimes accompanied on his journeys in the Maine woods. Ganong had also corresponded with Hardy on the distribution of animals in Maine and New Brunswick, the wolverine in particular. Fannie married

Fannie Hardy Eckstorm (1865–1946). MAINE FOLKLIFE CENTER: PO340

and settled in Brewer where, widowed early, she devoted the rest of her life to her two children and the lore and life of the Maine woods. She became an accomplished folklorist and ethnologist, writing a book, *Indian Place-Names of the Penobscot Valley and the Maine Coast*, published by the University of Maine in 1941. Although outspoken and never hesitating to correct Ganong, she generously conceded that her value to him lay not so much in what she knew but in what she could discover. As a fellow researcher, she acknowledged that Dr. Ganong's was "always the advice most valued." She and Ganong were born within a year of each other and for forty years were regular correspondents and in time firm friends. He once told her that "Brewer, Me." was his favourite postmark. Like Ganong, she was apprehensive about the loss of Aboriginal languages and names, noting repeatedly the narrowing window of time in which to record them and wishing that they had begun their collaboration twenty years earlier.

Ganong's other long-time collaborator in the matter of Aboriginal names was French-born Father Pacifique (Henri-Louis-Joseph Buisson), a missionary priest of the Capucin Monastery, Ste. Anne de Restigouche in Quebec and, according to Ganong, the most learned living authority on the Mi'kmaw language. Ganong and Father Pacifique's association began in 1902 when Father Pacifique asked by letter if he might borrow Ganong's list of Acadian-Mi'kmaw place names. He explained he worked with Mi'kmaq on the Restigouche and was learning their language, customs, and history.

They began to collaborate during the First World War when, at Ganong's request, Pacifique asked his older parishioners if they would list all the names they could think of on the Restigouche and its tributaries, from source to mouth. Three volunteered, and at the cost of a few piastres and food for the day, they provided two hundred names of places, tributary streams, rapids, waterfalls, and prominent features not just on the Restigouche but on the Matapedia, Patapedia, and the Uppsalquitch. It was the first list of many and the beginning of an almost thirty-year collaboration. Ganong and Pacifique had a regular—if not profuse—correspondence, Ganong writing in English and Father Pacifique replying in French.

The beginning, however, was very shaky: Ganong—his anti-clericalism showing—later wrote that he first had to convince Father Pacifique that his interpretations, unlike the Pope's, were not infallible. On his first list of interpreted names—almost every one of which Ganong declared "absolutely wrong"—Father Pacifique had written elaborately on the bottom: "I hereby certify that these explanations are strictly correct." Father Pacifique's command of Mi'kmaw, of which Ganong understood only the general principles, was greater than Ganong's, but in a letter to Fannie Eckstorm, Ganong avowed that he knew more of the "working gyrations" of the human mind and in tandem, they made a very good team.

Ganong wrote the foreword to Father Pacifique's 1934 book on Mi'kmaw place names and drew five of the maps. The two men met at least once, in Rothesay. In a letter to Fannie Eckstorm, Ganong described Pacifique as "a charming person, patriarchal, with a long flowing beard, brown robe, close skullcap—a scholar and a gentleman, deeply immersed in the spiritual and material welfare of his beloved Micmacs.... Just now he is going as deeply as he can into Micmac grammar—[he] knows the literature well."

Ganong's other Anglophone collaborators were Tappan Adney of Woodstock and Michael Flinne of Newcastle, on the Miramichi. Adney is best known as a historian and builder of Maliseet canoes, but he was also deeply interested in Maliseet culture. He spoke the language and he worked on a dictionary and grammar guide (never published) with Dr. Peter Paul of the Woodstock reserve. Adney's primary interest was in the origins and structure of the language, rather than geographical names, and although he was sometimes critical of Ganong's interpretations, Adney was "astonished" at the amount of research and complimented Ganong on his "great work." Like Ganong, he was aware of the pitfalls: "In place names the Indian tradition is broken, without which [there can be] no certainty of analysis." Transcriptions were often inexact and, as a result, the words much corrupted. The French invariably wrote *R* in place of the Indian *L* because the pronunciation of the French *L* and *R* do not differ as much as they do in English. They make, wrote Adney, a lateral "throat" *R* that evidently served for the Aboriginals' *L*.

Henri-Louis-Joseph Buisson (le Père Pacifique). New Brunswick Museum, Ganong
Collection: f64-1

Later, in an August 1950 letter to New Brunswick historian Lillian Maxwell, Adney reversed his earlier opinion of Ganong. Then in his early eighties, he was considering where he could safely place his research materials: "I must consider the disposition of a large accumulation of original research notes on [...] language and place names, and from this first critical revision the reflection is necessarily so severe on Ganong's mistranslations and misrepresentations of the facts of history of our Indians and of their language with which Ganong was singularly unacquainted, I have hesitated in filing such manuscripts with the NB Museum at St. John now that my staunch friend Dr. Webster is gone, lest my findings be suppressed." Adney considered his original "on the ground" researches to be "revolutionary," as they exposed "the astonishing errors of Ganong in analysis" and tried to solicit John Clarence Webster's support. Webster, who was a great friend and associate of Ganong's, replied noncommittally: "The work must continue. Let the chips fall where they may."

Michael Flinne, an unassuming schoolmaster and one of Ganong's earliest collaborators, began corresponding with him in the early 1890s when Ganong was still at Harvard. Rain or shine, Flinne walked almost five kilometres each way to school, which left little time or energy for Mi'kmaw studies. After a heavy snowfall it might be seven in the evening before he could settle down to read and write. Flinne, to whom Ganong sent a copy of Silas Rand's Mi'kmaw dictionary, was interested in the Mi'kmaw language and compiled a thirteen-letter phonetic alphabet of Miramichi Mi'kmaw. He calculated that their vocabulary amounted to three or four thousand words. For Ganong, Flinne was a source of place names and Indian lore, and, like Ganong, he was meticulous, always admitting when "a shadow of uncertainty" might cloud the information. "Certainty," he wrote in words that could only have reassured Ganong, "cannot be built upon uncertainty."

Information provided by living Aboriginals was indispensable but was always received with the caveat that it might be unreliable. Anxious to please, unlettered informants of whatever race or creed were always inclined, Ganong advised, to tell the investigator what he or she wanted to hear. One of Fannie Eckstorm's most frequent informants, eighty-four-year-old widow Clara Neptune (a Penobscot who supported herself and a great-grandson by making baskets, selling fortunes, and collecting folklore), was not above "cheating" her. Although "as sharp as a needle" and familiar with the mythology, legends, and beliefs of her people, she knew, according to Eckstorm, no more of the woods and waters than a Boston street gamin. "She is incredibly ignorant of both natural history and topography…. Clara's geography must be taken for what it is worth." Eckstorm, who paid Neptune small amounts, supplied Ganong with hundreds of traditional Aboriginal names and place names for which Ganong reimbursed her. She told Neptune that though she might occasionally cheat her, she could not fool the learned professor who spoke the language. "I have impressed upon her the all-seeing eye to which her stuff is to be exhibited." Neptune promised Eckstorm she would not make up anything. Newell Lyon sometimes did, she acknowledged, but she would not.

Eckstorm's other major informant was eighty-two-year-old Tobique-born Louis or Lewey Ketchum, a Penobscot who spoke good English and could get at the meanings of words more easily. Eckstorm used him to check on Neptune. One of Ganong's sources was also a Lewey: Noel Lewey from Pleasant Point in Perry, Maine, from whom after several days on the Schoodic lakes in 1912 he obtained "a rich harvest of names and other Indian matters." In December 1916 Noel Lewey wrote a pencilled note on lined paper wishing Ganong season's greetings and thanking him for the five-dollar cheque in exchange for providing names. He would also have provided names for Aboriginal stopping places, but he complained that none of his own informants could spell. He signed the letter "from your friend, Noel Lewey." The following year he sent more place names and promised photographs of his children: Cecelia, his sixteen-year-old second daughter; his boy, Lux, the fifth generation of that name; and one of his youngest boys, Athean, named after his grandfather.

Aboriginals who had heard of his search for names also approached Ganong independently. In 1925, Chief Jerry Lone Cloud, of the Nova Scotia Mi'kmaq, who professed a thorough knowledge of both the Mi'kmaw language and the province of Nova Scotia, sent him a list of a dozen names, promising more if they proved satisfactory. He also sent a photograph of himself (made into a postcard) and, as guarantor, the name of Harry Piers, the well-known curator of the Nova Scotia Museum for whom Lone Cloud was an important source for Mi'kmaw culture and language.

Like Fannie Eckstorm, Michael Flinne was also wary of Aboriginal sources. Although his chief local informant was reliable he was away in the woods for long periods at a time, and the resident Aboriginals (in general) were uninformed of things within their own locality that Flinne thought they ought to have known about. Few could help him with the interpretation of names that Ganong had sent him, and when teaching at Eel Ground, he found the residents of little help in his effort to learn the local dialect and grammar. They had no formal understanding of the structure of their language, making him rely almost entirely upon Silas Rand's *Dictionary* in his effort to master it.

Reliable First Nations sources were invaluable, but Ganong considered that on the question of names the conclusions of trained, disinterested language specialists on balance were safer provided they conducted field checks. In the Aboriginal languages of North America there were no proper names, that is, names that were mere marks (labels) devoid of meaning. Aboriginal names invariably described or were related to the place or locality to which they were attached even though changes in language and spelling might have obscured the original meaning. Usually, the name described the topography or physiography of the place, but it might refer to a well-known feast or a battle, or to the availability of food, water, or shelter, or to animals that inhabited or frequented it.

First Nations informants could be so unreliable that Ganong described one of his own chief sources of names, Jim Paul, as "an awful liar unless checked." Paul's saving grace was that "he knows a lot," and as Ganong told Fannie Eckstorm, the "lying" didn't matter as he (Ganong) was adept at disentangling interlayered fact and fiction. Tappan Adney was also wary of Aboriginal informants and to avoid "guesswork," he seldom asked them the meaning of anything. He asked instead if they could recall the context in which particular words might have been used. Adney encouraged Ganong's scientific, non-speculative approach to Aboriginal languages by citing Ernest Renan, the renowned nineteenth-century

Halifax, Dec. 20, 1925.

Mr. W. M. Ganong,
   305 Prospect Heights,
      Northampton, Mass., U. S. A.

Dear Sir:

     I have heard that you wish to get in touch with someone
who can translate Indian names.

     I am Chief of the Micmacs in Nova Scotia and have a thorough
knowledge of the Micmac language.

     If you wish confirmation as to my ability, I refer you to Mr.
Harry Piers, Halifax Museum, Halifax, Nova Scotia.

     Kindly let me hear from you as soon as possible,   Address,--
Chief Lonecloud, Armdale Post Office, Armdale, Halifax, Nova Scotia,
Canada.

               Yours truly,

               Chief Lone Cloud

A letter from Chief Jerry Lone Cloud to Ganong, offering help with his place-names research. He enclosed a postcard of himself with his grandson, 1925. New Brunswick Museum, Ganong Collection: F23-8 (1 & 2)

Armdale, Halifax Co.,

Feb. 19, 1926.

Wm. F. Ganong,
        Smith's College,
                Northampton, Mass., U. S.

Dear Sir:

        Your letter should have been answered ere this but it
lay in the post office for some time, owing to my absence from the
city.

        Naturally I know a great many Indian names.   I am enclosing
you a dozen as a sample and hope they will be satisfactory.

        I am thoroughly familiar with all parts of Nova Scotia.

                        Yours truly,

                        Chief Lone Cloud

A follow-up letter from Chief Jerry Lone Cloud, 1926. NEW BRUNSWICK MUSEUM, GANONG
COLLECTION: F23-8 (3)

French philologist. Renan believed that only through rigorous scientific analysis could language be understood, and once understood it shed light on the relations of its authors with the external world. Anthropologist Franz Boas in the 1930s declared place nomenclature to be an avenue to the understanding of culture.

In four long articles for the TRSC, Ganong chose more than thirty place names, some extant and some extinct, with strong, unambiguous roots that might serve as platforms for the analysis of related names. The extinct names might be revived when additional place names were needed. In each case he adopted a standard approach. So that the articles might be read and understood by all readers, he dispensed with specialized alphabets devised by linguists to represent sounds, in favour of the familiar English alphabet whose letters he combined to replicate phonetically the sound of the words. In certain cases, however, there were sounds for which English had no equivalent.

He began each investigation with a history of the word from its earliest appearance in documents and maps, presenting in great detail the various spellings to which it had been subjected. He followed this with an analysis of the possible meanings of the word itself, based upon dictionaries—primarily Rand's Mi'kmaw–English dictionary—and interviews with trusted First Nations informants. All but a few of the names are of Mi'kmaw origin. One of the revelations of the study is that the Mi'kmaw domain—previously thought to have been the Atlantic coast—had once extended down to the coast of the Bay of Fundy to the lower St. John, and into Maine. Because most of the names would be related to some physical characteristic of the place, it was essential that investigators become thoroughly acquainted with the places in question. This was the third and final stage. According to Ganong, the three-stage approach had not been used anywhere else in Canada.

To begin his analysis of names in his third paper, Ganong chose Oromocto, a river tributary to the St. John in south-central New Brunswick. In early French maps and documents it is spelled Ramoucto or Le Ramoucto. In early English sources it is variously Ramatou, Ramaucta, and Ramactou. In 1786, George Sproule, surveyor general for New Brunswick, used Oromocto, establishing the standard spelling.

Newell Paul, one of Ganong's most reliable Aboriginal informants, pronounced it Welamoogtook from which both French and English versions were derived.

Ganong met Newell Paul in 1889 at a Maliseet reserve on his Woolastook trip and found him to be the most intelligent and best-informed Aboriginal source he had ever met. Paul spoke excellent English, and Ganong, as was his habit, drained him of information on the place names, legends, and customs of his people. Newell Paul translated Oromocto as "handsome river," or a river that "looks very well indeed." Since neither the Maliseet nor the Mi'kmaq seemed to have had any conception of scenery or aesthetic of place unconnected with utility, Ganong opted for a prosaic interpretation. For the first nineteen kilometres of its course from the St. John to the forks, the Oromocto is a sedate river, "a winding deadwater stream of the gentlest character." For

Ganong's sketch of his audience with Newell Paul, a knowledgeable and reliable Maliseet informant, 1889. NEW BRUNSWICK MUSEUM, GANONG COLLECTION: F455-18L

Aboriginals, this translated to easy navigation or easy canoeing. Although the Oromocto is now in Maliseet territory, the investigation revealed that the word is actually of Mi'kmaw origin. The Mi'kmaq applied exactly the same name, Welamoogtook, to what is now the Cains River, a large branch of the Miramichi with a leisurely current in the lower half of its course, broken only by gentle rapids.

In the case of the Magaguadavic, a river that flows into the Bay of Fundy at St. George, a resource determined the name. According to Newell Paul, the word was a derivation of Mag-e-Gad-a-Vic, a Mi'kmaw word meaning "big eel place." Eels were a prized fish, so large in the Magaguadavic that First Nations were able to spear them. Three kilometres above the fall of the river, at St. George, the Magaguadavic is a deadwater, a condition prized by eels. From Tappan Adney, Ganong learned that the name Magaguadavic might refer to the eels' habit in some places of tying themselves into tight bunches as big as a peck measure, with ends wriggling: "Mek-Muk-Mug" means close together in Mi'kmaw. Because he found the Anglicized spelling Magaguadavic "cumbersome," Ganong suggested a change to Macadayvee or Macadavie. Railroad men abbreviated it to M'Davy. For suggesting the change, Ganong, as pointed out earlier, was rounded on by James Vroom, a local historian and the town clerk and treasurer of St. Stephen.

When he could not get help with the origins of names from living Mi'kmaq, Ganong turned, in the light of what he described as the "genius of Indian name-giving," to physiography. A case in point was the Sevogle, a tributary of the Northwest Miramichi. The course of the river is distinguished by a series of interglacial and postglacial gorges with vertical cliff walls. The Mi'kmaw word for cliffs is *sok* and the Mi'kmaw name for the river was Sewokul. Thus the corrupted form, Sevogle, indicated a river of many cliffs. In the same vein, Upsalquitch, the name for a branch of the Restigouche, signified small or lesser river. In Mi'kmaw the root *apsak* signifies small, and *kwek*, the root of *quetch*, a minor river or stream. The Upsalquitch, however, is small only in relation to the Restigouche into which it flows. In southeast New Brunswick the Petitcodiac, a derivation of Pet-koot-koy-ek, is a Mi'kmaw word signifying a river that bends around in a bow or bends around and back on itself. A remarkable feature of the Petitcodiac is that in its lower course it performs a double bend that gives it a flat *S* form. Ganong dismissed as fanciful Moses Perley's version of a French origin, and the one commonly adopted, of *petite coude* (little elbow).

Each of the thirty or so primary names in Ganong's articles is subjected to several pages of close-printed, meticulous, detailed historical and etymological analysis. My summaries of just a few of them are severe abbreviations. The complete versions will engage the trained philologist but might exhaust the lay reader. They are a demonstration of Ganong's mantra that in scientific and historical research accuracy is more important than brevity.

THE FRENCH

Ganong's interests in the First Nations and the French nourished each other. Through their trade in furs and their successful Catholic missions, French relations with the First Nations were cordial and amply recorded. In 1908 Ganong translated and edited, for the Champlain Society, Nicolas Denys's seventeenth-century narrative, *The Description and Natural History of the Coasts of North America*. He followed this in 1910 with a translation of Father Chrétien Le Clercq's *Nouvelle Relation de la Gaspésie*. In 1929 he also translated (with H. H. Langton) Champlain's narratives of his voyages in the St. Lawrence and the Bay of Fundy (Volume 3 of Champlain's collected works).

The translations of the Denys and Le Clercq narratives were labours only a devotee of the province's or Maritime history would have undertaken. Both books were written in old French, unfamiliar to Ganong, and to translate the Denys narrative he enlisted the aid of Mademoiselle Vincens, Professor of French at Smith. For bibliographic work, he appealed to his friend Victor Hugo Paltsits, the New York librarian and archivist. Even more trying than the medium was the manner of the message. Denys wrote the most ungainly, leaden prose—eight hundred pages of it in two volumes. He was, according to Ganong, without imagination and humour, and oblivious to beauty. As translator and editor, Ganong not only had to convert bad French into good English (it was commendably readable prose) but to correct factual errors and clarify what was obscure. Denys wrote his book (ca. 1671) from memory some thirty years after his arrival in Nova Scotia. Ganong conceded that only a translator with local knowledge of the places described and collateral knowledge of events and contemporary records bearing on Denys's narrative could have managed it. Yet the exercise energized rather than exhausted him: "I consider this one of the greatest pieces of good fortune of my life that this work had not earlier been done, and that there has fallen to me the highly congenial task of translating and editing this important book, devoted to country and to subjects that interest me so much." He told Paltsits he even considered cruising around the coasts of Cape Breton and Nova Scotia to familiarize himself with the places mentioned by Denys, resorting to his bicycle if necessary. He was already familiar with most of the New Brunswick sites.

Ganong's interest in Denys dated from his brief teaching spell at the Natural History Society of Worcester, Massachusetts, in 1885. In a notebook labelled "Myology," devoted largely to drawings of the muscular and skeletal structures of a cat and birds, Ganong had copied paragraphs on shellfish from Denys's 1632 narrative. Ganong copied the French, and a friend or colleague provided a translation in English on the facing page. The name Cocagne (the mythic medieval land of ease and plenty) that Denys applied to one of the North Shore harbours was no doubt inspired by the abundance of finfish, but the decisive fact may well have been the wealth of shellfish near the shore. The claws of some of the lobsters were large enough to hold a pint of wine, and the flesh, eaten with a variety of sauces, was so full and rich that they called them the partridges of the sea. Oysters, taken from coves by breaking the ice, were the great "manna" of winter when sea fishing was not possible. They were caught with long thin poles tied together in such a way that they behaved liked tongs, placed on the ice, opened and drained, sprinkled with bread crumbs, seasoned with nutmeg and pepper, and then cooked in large shells on hot coals. They made a very good feast.

Although Acadia was not a particular interest of Fannie Eckstorm's, she admired Ganong's translation. In response to an enthusiastic letter from her, he wrote: "So you have found my Denys, I took lots of satisfaction about it. I have never cared whether anybody else read it or not...it interested me so much that that was enough." To the six-hundred-page text, Ganong appended a nineteen-page bibliography that included, in his own words, the title of every known publication and manuscript containing original information about Denys, or distinctive matter bearing on his life.

Denys was born in Tours, France, in 1598 and came to Nova Scotia in 1632. He was a businessman with interests in the cod fishery and the fur trade, and by the mid-seventeenth century he had established trading stations at Rossignol, near Liverpool, Nova Scotia, and at Miscou and Nepisiguit (Bathurst). In 1653 he became the proprietor of the mainland and islands between Canso and Gaspé, and a year later he received letters patent from the King appointing him Governor and Lieutenant General of the same territory. His life ended in penury, however, and he devoted large sections of his book to deriding the characters of those he believed had injured or ruined him. The saving grace of the book for Ganong was that the rest is a trove of information about life and work in seventeenth-century Acadia. Presentation didn't matter to Denys, and it mattered even less to Ganong. Denys seems to have had little education and by his own admission took little joy in composition. Ganong was unfazed, pleased even that Denys's narrative would be baldly factual: "If he had no goodness of style, he had that which is far better: something of value to say." Denys, Ganong added, could do things well even if he could not tell them well. Denys abhorred "loud talkers and promoters" even though when it came to the country he adopted he was not above a little promotion himself.

Denys, and this must have endeared him to Ganong, had abounding faith in coastal Acadia, and like the authors of immigration handbooks he magnified its virtues and minimized its faults. With ample wood, good harbours, and unlimited quantities of fish, the living was relatively easy, the climate, in the same latitudes as France, was not so very different from the homeland, and the cold was not excessive. It was also closer to France than coastal areas to the south. Not only this, settlers would be able to grow the same fruits, grains, and vegetables as they did at home. It was, said Ganong, the first Acadian and Canadian immigration tract.

The most valuable chapters in the book are those that describe the cod fishery in—Ganong's phrase—pre-Raphaelite detail. Denys was a master fisherman and probably learned his trade as a fishing apprentice on transatlantic expeditions from the Normandy ports. So rich was the North Shore fishery that he named one of its harbours Cocagne, after the mythic medieval land of ease and plenty. Each spring and summer several hundred vessels sailed from western and northwestern France to fish in the waters off Acadia. Denys's 200-page account of the summer fishery was the first, justifying the prodigious and marvellous detail. Fannie Eckstorm remarked how unusual it was for anyone to write down what he knew about a particular trade with enough detail that the next generation would fully understand the process. The account begins with the making and marking of sections of new fishing boats in France that were then loaded onto larger vessels for reassembly on arrival, and ends with the return of dried and salted fish to France, much of it for the Paris market. Each procedure is described in a short and, despite Ganong's disclaimers, engrossing chapter. On arrival in Acadia, carpenters and crews assembled the boats and built workstations and wooden stages for handling and drying the fish, and summer lodgings for the men, using sails for roofing and the interlaced branches of fir and spruce for protective walls. Under the supervision of a beach master, the fish were dried and stacked in windmill-shaped piles before loading. Oil extracted from the livers was stored in barrels and sent back to France in ships packed from bow to stern with dried and salted fish.

In matters of baiting, handlining from small boats, gutting, splitting, and salting the caught fish, no detail was overlooked. The splitters then, as later, wore long protective aprons or barvels. Denys also described the policing system used by the captains to avoid congestion and friction when so many boats pursued the same quarry in restricted waters and two distinctive ways of preserving and marketing the fish. In one, the fish were split and salted on the vessel itself and taken back to France in a semi-cured state. In the other "sedentary" method, drying was completed ashore before the return to France. The sedentary method required larger crews and the division of the hands into those who caught the fish and those who processed them ashore. As a description of the fishery, only Moses Perley's account, written more than two hundred years later, would compare with it, and this distantly.

Denys was just as painstaking in his account of the Mi'kmaq, describing their dress, games, rituals, customs, dwellings, diet, domestic life, and methods of hunting. Bows, knives, arrows, spears, and the ways of making and using them are described in intricate detail. Until their contact with Europeans, the Mi'kmaq lived well, but brandy, which they obtained from French fishermen and traders in exchange for furs and skins, wreaked havoc. This, too, Denys described in detail.

Father Le Clercq's six-hundred-page book might have been of less interest to Ganong, but he also regarded the translation of it as a privilege. As a Recollet missionary, Le Clercq ministered for twelve years in Mi'kmaw settlements between Gaspé and the Miramichi. He quickly learned the dialect and devised a system of hieroglyphics that enabled the Mi'kmaq to learn the prayers, chants, and tenets of the Catholic faith. He recorded every aspect of Aboriginal life and customs, leaving, like Denys, invaluable details of dress, diet, dwellings, and hunting practices. For Ganong, Le Clercq's finest writing was on Mi'kmaw domestic life: "Nowhere does our literature offer a finer picture of the family life of the Indians."

When working on the translation of Denys's narrative, Ganong had difficulty identifying some of the plants and animals mentioned by him. For help, he turned to the writings of other sixteenth- and seventeenth-century voyagers and chroniclers who had travelled or sojourned in the same region and noted the names of the plants and animals cited. He compared usages and then compiled a key, an annotated listing or inventory, forty pages long, of all the animals and plants that had drawn the attention of the voyagers. He called it a "Dictionary of Identities of Animals and Plants." Published by the Royal Society in 1909, it has 331 entries ranging in length from a sentence to a full paragraph, each entry citing works in which the name occurs. The list begins with "aigle, aigrette" (the French name for crested heron used first by Lescarbot and Denys) and "alder," and ends with "verdière" (the French name for the greenfinch of Europe but transferred to Acadia's black-throated green warbler) and "vigne," first used by Cartier in 1534. To avoid scientific nomenclature, which dissenting scientists kept in a near constant state of flux, Ganong used common names—which he thought more stable and distinctive—throughout.

He also identified stages in the process of naming. For species found on both sides of the Atlantic, early voyagers simply applied generic European names, either French (*ours, loups, outres*) or English (bears, wolves, otters). For species similar to the European but for which Europe had no exact representative, they selected the closest match. Thus rabbit for our hare, robin for our thrush, partridge for our grouse, *outarde* for the Canada goose, and *rossignol* for our song sparrow. For species that had no close European relatives they adopted Aboriginal names. Ganong's examples are caribou, moose, carcajou (wolverine), *chicamin* (ground nut or Indian potato) and *pounamon* (tomcod). Finally, there are names that appear to have been inventions, possibly accidental, of explorers and fishermen for which there are no identifiable origins. Examples include: *mermette, gode, esterlet,* and *marionette.* Ganong made no claim for the species list, which appears to have been exhaustive, other than it might serve as a useful basis for further study of an interesting subject.

Ganong's interest in Acadians embraced both their historic and current settlements. He was the first to write a history of the founding Acadian settlement on St. Croix Island and the first English historian to write detailed accounts of the post-Expulsion settlements on the North Shore. For a keynote speaker at the tercentenary celebration of the 1604 Champlain settlement, Ganong, an eminent New Brunswick scholar working in the United States, was an obvious choice. James Vroom of St. Stephen was the local secretary for the celebration. St. Croix Island is on the US side of the border, and the chosen venue for the address was the opera house in Calais, Maine. Ganong began his talk, "The Meaning of the Day," by noting that the landing and subsequent settlement on the island led to the foundation of Acadia and the temporary rule of France in North America. It was the first European settlement on the continent above the Spanish settlements in Florida and the Gulf of Mexico. He followed this with praise for Sieur de Monts, the commander of the company, and for Samuel de Champlain, its incomparable cartographer and chronicler. Although short-lived—the company removed to Port Royal across the Bay of Fundy the following summer—the settlement and the diminutive island, 6.5 acres in size, were the keys to the amicable solution of the international boundary dispute between Great Britain and the United States. The island, Ganong concluded, is "one of those rare places where the thoughtful student may come into communion with the silent witness of history."

His earlier 1902 monograph, "Dochet (St. Croix) Island," for the TRSC was a comprehensive history of the island and the settlement. Revised and enlarged by his sister Susan, the New Brunswick Museum reprinted it as a book, *Ste. Croix (Dochet) Island*, in 1945. Ganong had known the island since boyhood. In the monograph, his objective had been "to set forth, accurately, fully, and clearly…all that is known of [its] history." In his review for the *American Historical Review*, Victor Hugo Paltsits expressed his wonder that "for a seemingly unimportant island today, Dr. Ganong has succeeded in bringing together a mass of historical data sufficient to make a monograph of about one hundred closely printed octavo pages appropriately illustrated and enhanced by a new survey."

In retrospect, a small island in the middle of a large river might seem an odd location for a permanent settlement, but there was room enough

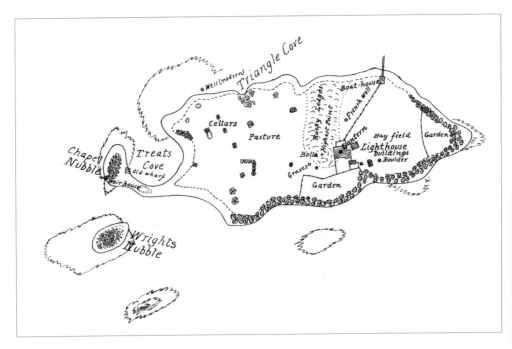

Ganong's 1903 sketch map of the French settlement on St. Croix Island, made after his survey of the island. NEW BRUNSWICK MUSEUM, GANONG COLLECTION: F499-7

for buildings and gardens, and the island could easily be defended against European usurpers and potentially hostile Aboriginals. Fuel and water, they thought (not unreasonably), could be brought from the mainland. The island soil, however, proved very sandy, and the crops burned up in the dry, hot summer. As a safeguard, De Monts had gardens dug on the mainland in what Ganong concluded was the sheltered cove below the falls at St. Stephen. On their own shore they found plenty of clams, mussels, sea urchins, and sea snails.

Their plans and precautions, however, were undone by a fierce winter and scurvy. They had no fresh fruit, vegetables, or juices during the winter months (and no awareness of the indispensability of vitamin C) and their meat was salted. Disarmed by the heat of summer and unaware of the limitations of latitude as a determinant of climate, they had no expectations of an unbearably cold winter; St. Croix Island is on the same latitude as Bordeaux. It was also a period of unusual cold, the Little Ice Age, when canals and rivers in London and Amsterdam froze regularly. On the St. Croix the first snow fell on October 6, and on December 3 ice floes passed the island. Once frozen, the river ice was so fractured by winds and tides that fuel could not be hauled from the mainland. By the following spring, thirty-four of the party of seventy-nine had died and the survivors began preparations for a move across the bay to Port Royal in Nova Scotia where, according to Champlain, the climate was more agreeable.

For the post-Expulsion Acadian settlements on the North Shore, Ganong planned a series of twelve articles for *Acadiensis* but completed only eight of them (Miscou, Tracadie, Caraquet, Pokemouche, Shippegan, Tabusintac, Neguac, and Burnt Church) before the journal folded. As in his Aboriginal place name studies, he was driven by the evanescence of memory and the need to record those memories that remained. "It happens that the most important phase of the history of them all, that which concerns the founding of the modern settlements, is almost wholly unrecorded, and exists only in the memories or traditions of the older residents. It is my aim to collect the essential facts while there is time, and to preserve them for future generations of New Brunswick men and women who will care for these things."

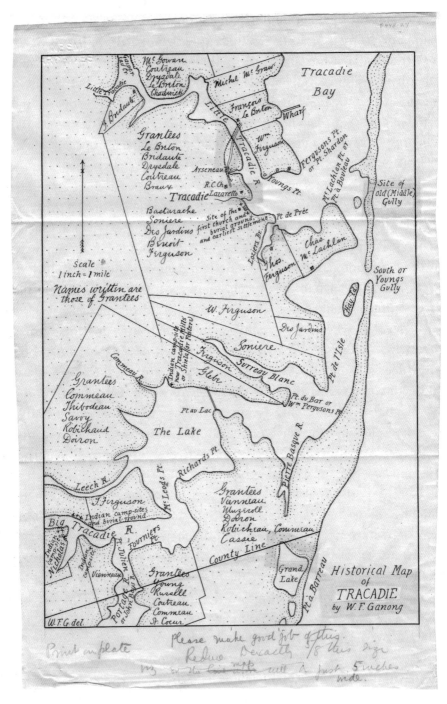

Ganong's map of historical Tracadie. NEW BRUNSWICK MUSEUM, GANONG COLLECTION: F448-24

He began with a description of the location and topography of each place and followed this with an outline of the origins and early history with (unusual in history journals) as much detail of the names and families of the early settlers as he could gather, aware that the information would interest descendants. He provided full references to the published material relating to each settlement, but most of the information on the modern settlements came from the residents themselves and from local historians, not published works. To unearth the latter he elicited the aid of the archivist Victor Hugo Paltsits.

Following the lead of the trader and traveller Gamaliel Smethurst, whose 1774 account of his escape from the Mi'kmaq Ganong had edited, he advised the reader, quoting Smethurst, that his aim was to instruct not entertain: "[to] have no concern save to set down clearly that which I believe to be true." Smethurst had preferred "simple truths" over the embellishments and colourings of the best writers. Victor Hugo Paltsits, however, suggested in a note to Ganong that the hazards attending Smethurst's escape might not have been much greater than those that usually attended travel and navigation in a northern climate during winter.

Ganong began with Miscou, the most remote of the North Shore settlements at the entrance to Chaleur Bay, and one which, from his studies of plant succession on the beach plain, he knew well. The name Miscou itself is a derivation of a Mi'kmaw word (*m'susqu*) meaning low or wet ground; great moors of bog barrens make up half the island. The first Europeans to arrive were Jesuit missionaries and traders interested in furs and fish, and the oil and ivory of the sea cow or walrus, which they pursued and hunted to extinction in the Atlantic region. Among the early permanent settlers was Nicholas Denys who in 1652 established a trading post as well as "a pleasant garden." Vulnerable to attack, Miscou was probably abandoned by the French during the Seven Years' War, after which control of the country passed to England. Formerly exiled and outlawed Acadians began to return around 1770 and joined, or were joined by, Scots who may have come to Miramichi in returning lumber vessels from Great Britain. On the island they cut wild hay and raised cattle. Other early arrivals were Jersey merchants who established a fishery station at Miscou Point and obtained a grant of the north end of the island. Jersey merchants were prominent in the life and commerce of the North Shore settlements. Random settlement by disparate groups was, according to Ganong, characteristic of the North Shore.

Before 1860 the settlement at Miscou was entirely coastal, but the building of a road through good upland in the southwest part of the island attracted farmers. The official name for the more inland settlement was Miscou Centre, but because of its linear nature it was known locally as "The Road." On the island there was some mingling of English and French, but those at Miscou Point were largely English while those at Miscou Centre and Grande Plaine were entirely French. The French were

The Silvas family home in Grande Plaine, Gloucester County, 1923. NEW BRUNSWICK MUSEUM, GANONG COLLECTION: 1987-17-1222-41

increasing more rapidly, and it seemed inevitable that there, as elsewhere, they would eventually outnumber the English. To sum up, Ganong characterized the Miscou man as a fisherman who farms a little in the intervals and whose lack of education and remoteness have kept him poor. "Though circumstances have thus been hard for him, he has, in one way, risen above them for I have found him always, whether English or French, content, healthy, kindly, and hospitable."

The other North Shore villages he treated in a similar fashion, beginning with the initial Mi'kmaw settlements, then the arrival of the Europeans and the ways in which they sustained themselves. As at Miscou, settlement was random. Acadians began to arrive after the peace between England and France; Scots and English came either directly from Scotland or from America at the end of the Revolutionary War. Their descendants spoke French rather than English, and many of them became Catholic. Among the Scots were 42nd Highlanders who had been assigned lands on the Nashwaak. Not satisfied with their holdings they moved down the Miramichi and made their way to settlements on the North Shore. All the settlements practiced a mixed farming/fishing economy supplemented by resources particular to the place. Tabusintac had hemlock and immense quantities of pure peat that Ganong thought was certain to be of great value one day. It was settled late after more favourable locations were taken. Shippegan, founded by Nicolas Denys in 1645, was probably settled by Norman French from the north side of Chaleur Bay and joined by English businessmen who came to conduct business with the fishermen. These anchored at Shippegan and dried their fish on an island nearby. Tracadie was settled first by Acadians in 1785 followed by English and sundry settlers from older settlements seeking new locations for farming and fishing. The country around had white pine, and soils that could be farmed "with profit but not to affluence." Pokemouche had a poor harbour and no fishery but abundant lumber (white pine) and a fair soil so that the Pokemouche man, Ganong wrote, is a lumberman in winter, a farmer in summer, a sportsman in the autumn, and a fisherman at odd times.

The most distinctive of the villages, and the one that appealed to Ganong most, was Caraquet. He loved the twenty-two-kilometre-long settlement on an inlet toward the eastern end of Chaleur Bay. "Somehow in summer all the distance seems to glow with softest blue, the sea, the sky, the distant Gaspe hills; while all the line of shore and island and forest breathe the very air of quiet peace and rest." Caraquet was first settled by a solitary Frenchman in the 1720s. In his 1764 narrative of his escape from the Mi'kmaq (edited by Ganong), Gamaliel Smethurst refers to a Frenchman from Old France who had been living in Caraquet for decades and had taken a Mi'kmaw wife. Greater settlement by Europeans had to await the arrival of Acadians after the Expulsion. An unpublished document in the Paris Archives, dated 1760, named thirty-six families at Caraquet, but most were probably driven off by the English. After the peace of 1763 two distinct settlements developed: Acadians settled in what is now Upper Caraquet, the western half of the shoreline village that stretches the length of Caraquet Bay, while Normans and Canadiens settled in Lower Caraquet. The Normans were primarily fishermen who had married Aboriginal women. From earliest times, according to Nicolas Denys, Pabos, Paspebiac, and Gaspé across the bay had been favourite bad-weather refuges for Norman fishermen. Canadiens came from different parts of Quebec. Unlike the other North Shore settlements,

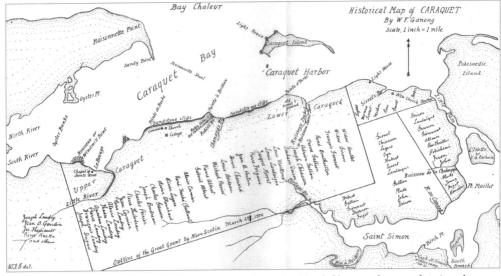

Ganong's map of historical Caraquet, his favourite North Shore settlement, showing the holdings of Acadian, Norman (French), and Canadien (Quebec) settlers.

ACADIENSIS, VOL. 7, NO. 2

Caraquet was wholly French in origin. For fifty years there was no evidence of intermarriage between Acadians and Normans/Canadiens. Scots, Englishmen, and Jerseymen eventually arrived, but many of these moved away leaving few descendants. The affectionate ending was one he applied to all his portraits of the North Shore settlements: "I like it much and I wish it well."

Ganong's affection for Acadians, then a neglected sector of the population, was demonstrated again in 1930 when he approached the New Brunswick Historical Society to publish Placide Gaudet's address to the Acadian Convention at Moncton in 1928. Gaudet was a renowned genealogist and historian who fell extremely ill in 1930. Ganong recommended that the simply and gracefully written article be published in French. Its quality alone merited acceptance, but publication by an Anglophone provincial society would also be "a generous gesture to our French fellow citizens."

Chapter 10

⠀⠀⠀⠀⠀⠀⠀⠀*ᘔᘔ ᘔᘔ*

COASTAL SUBSIDENCE

On his 1905 canoe trip with Arthur Pierce that ended at Miscou, Ganong referred to the chain of lagoons and islands that follow the North Shore. He was intrigued; the chain began at Miscou and, in sinuous curves that parallel the shore, extended south as far as Buctouche. In 1906 Ganong presented his observations to the NHSNB, and in the 1908 *Bulletin* he published a two-part article on their physical geography that combined lyrical descriptions of the islands with a clear exposition of the forces that shaped them. It was one of his most engaging publications, and it went far beyond the matter-of-fact requirements of physical geography.

The North Shore is gently sloping lowland, drained by rivers occupying broad shallow valleys that once accommodated much larger streams. Where the valleys meet the sea there are large in-bowed coves sheltered from the open ocean by the sand islands. Toward the sea, the islands (known locally as Beaches) present a moderate, smooth, hard slope where they are constantly pounded by wind and waves. On the landward side the slope is more gentle, clothed at its upper end by waving beach grass and at the lower by a close, fine, swale-like turf and still lower by a close salt marsh that dips imperceptibly into the waters of the lagoons between the islands and the coast. All are quite treeless, the sparse beach grass intermixed in sheltered places with low clumps of wax myrtle, *Hudsonia*, dwarf roses, sweet gale, and a few rarer plants of "humble habit." The descriptions are a touching reminder that Ganong first and foremost was a botanist.

The grasses, like those of the salt marshes, were sometimes cut for hay and sometimes used as pasture for horses and cattle. In this way, Ganong wrote, the Beaches "yield a small tribute to man." The fisheries offered a much larger tribute: salmon, following the coast, were caught in nets, and lobsters were trapped just off the shore. The buildings serving the fisheries were small huts, sometimes scattered, but more often clustered around the gullies that separated the islands and gave rivers access to the sea. From a distance, and especially in certain quiet hazy states of the atmosphere, the low-lying beaches seemed to sink from view, and the grey buildings appear to float mirage-like upon the waters. The low, grey line of distant Beaches, the weathered buildings, the distant roar of billows on the outer beach, the murmur of wind in the beach grass, and the screaming of gulls over the still lagoon gave a feeling of peace and contentment. They were the "character-feelings" of the Beach country. To some, the Beaches may have seemed dreary and without charm, but they had ample attraction "for those who love strong and simple things and the open places of the earth."

The lagoons, between the islands and the mainland, are shallow with bottoms of sandy mud that support a great growth of saltwater eel grass. Because they are sheltered, and because of the calming effect of the eel grass, they are always smooth no matter how hard the winds may blow or how roughly the sea breaks on the coast just outside them. Safe passage made the lagoons great canoe routes for the First Nations and led an early voyager, Gamaliel Smethurst in 1761, to describe them as the finest conveniences possible for canoes. Ganong agreed, having sailed his canoe in "happy safety" under a wind that strove to tear the sail from its fastenings and raised roaring surges upon the beaches outside. On his 1905 trip with Arthur Pierce, Ganong canoed down the Tracadie River to its mouth, keeping to the shore through the lagoon bays, sometimes sailing the canoe, and after ascending the tideway of the Pokemouche to its head, went through Shippagan harbour and along the north side of

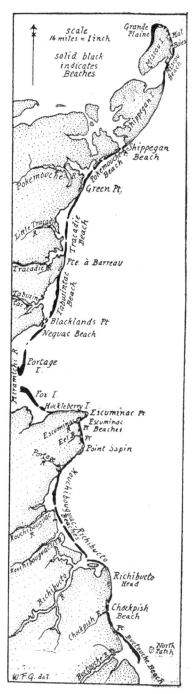

Sketch map of the sinuous North Shore sand islands or beaches whose origins intrigued Ganong. NEW BRUNSWICK MUSEUM, GANONG COLLECTION: NHS-V26-24

the islands to Grande Plaine in Miscou. There they made a base camp for study of the island, returning along the north shore to Caraquet. A year later, Ganong went with his brother Walter to the upper Tabusintac, descended that river by canoe, and followed the lagoon bays to Shediac, ascending the tideways of most of the rivers.

Ganong, of course, was never content to just appreciate form. He surmised that the islands originated as dunes or ridges upon a sinking mainland and that as the land sank beneath the water, the dunes, separated from the mainland, became islands. Wind and waves may have driven the islands inland, but that action was unable to keep up with the rising sea levels that invaded the land behind the dunes and formed lagoons. Because of continued subsidence, there would have been a general tendency for the islands, stabilized by grasses, to move outward rather than inward, perceptually. Sand carried through the gullies into the lagoons would be deposited as sandbars and shoals, forming the nuclei of an inner line of islands. To explain their parallelism to the coast, Ganong suggested if each island had a trailing end, not fixed by grasses, then wind and waves would plane off the sand and create a long curve concave to the shore. To conclude the article, he noted that the coast was still sinking, and the islands were still travelling slowly inward but at a slower rate than the sinking, retreating coastline. He described them as remarkably mobile phenomena that were among the most living and interesting of geographical features.

For Ganong, Grande Plaine, the subject of a contemporaneous study on the west side of Miscou Island, also offered convincing evidence of subsidence and demonstrated how some of the other islands farther down the coast might have looked before the sea separated them from the mainland. On Grande Plaine, the concentric ridges of the extensive sand plain became progressively lower as one moved inland. The progression was so marked that the entire plain had a pronounced inward slope, clear evidence, he asserted, of subsidence that led to a settling of water toward the older inner parts and a relatively higher water table. At the north end of the plain, the abrupt cliffs formed by waves cutting into the exposed ends of the dunes were also characteristic of a sinking shore.

To the south, in the Miramichi estuary, Ganong found that other islands, Portage Island in particular, bore a striking resemblance to Grande Plaine. Portage, too, was formed of a series of concentric low dune beaches, against neighbouring upland, with shallow hollows of salt marsh between the dunes. The beach lines formed only above the reach of the highest tides, and their gradual disappearance beneath the waters of the bay, Ganong asserted, was evidence of progressive subsidence along the coast. Submerged peat beds near the north end of the island offered further evidence of submergence as did the rapid erosion of materials that, as at Grande Plaine, were deposited at the southern end of the island. The whole island, as a result, appeared to be rolling southward along its outer margin. All the facts, Ganong concluded, seemed to indicate that Portage Island, like Grande Plaine, had formed against a neighbouring upland and that continued sinking had taken the land below the surface of the lagoon. In his thesis, Michael Caron pointed out that Ganong's extended comparison of the two islands was the most singular feature of his barrier island studies.

Ganong's interest in coastal submergence dated from his late-1880s studies of puzzling anomalies in the distribution of marine invertebrates in the Bay of Fundy. He published his findings in a major article, "Southern invertebrates on the shores of Acadia," in an 1890 issue of the *Transactions* of the RSC, while he was still at Harvard. In an earlier study, in the 1870s, C. J. Verrill had investigated an outlier of southern warm water species in Quahog Bay at the northern end of Casco Bay in Maine. The waters of the Bay of Fundy are generally cold. Verrill contended that the slow submergence of the Le Have and St. George's banks off the coast of Newfoundland had nullified their role as giant barriers to the Labrador current, allowing the cold waters to invade warm southern regions. Warm water species survived only in locally protected areas such as Quahog Bay.

In support of Verrill's theory, Ganong devoted three pages of his southern invertebrates paper to a review of the geological evidence for subsidence presented by geologists working in the Maritimes and the North Atlantic. Subsidence of the Atlantic coast had been documented since the 1850s when G. H. Cook of Rutgers College, after an exhaustive study, concluded that much of the New Jersey and northeast Atlantic coast was subsiding at a rate of about one foot per century.

In 1861, Abraham Gesner published a widely read study of vertical movements in North America. Gesner, like Ganong, had walked or canoed along much of the New Brunswick coastline and reported subsidence in several locations. Support also came from other notable geologists, among them R. W. Ells, R. M. Chalmers, and J. W. Dawson, the founding president of the Royal Society of Canada.

In the same paper, Ganong listed the geologic and cultural evidence supporting subsidence. From his own investigations he pointed to submerged tree stumps at Grand Manan and Manawoganish beach near Saint John and to banks of peat, composed of freshwater plants, now below high tide levels, being washed away by the sea. Submerged shell middens, burial grounds, and portage paths were commonplace, and he endorsed Gesner's observations of submerged military corduroy roads and the submergence of the causeway by tides at high water at old Fort Moncton. Ganong's 1890s peat bog studies and those of the salt marshes at the head of Bay of Fundy strongly suggested that the coast was sinking. There was also cartographic evidence. Maps of the North Shore by Humeau in 1685, by Franquelin de Meulles in 1686, and one earlier by an unknown surveyor, all show the presence of small islands lying off the eastern entrances of both the Miscou and Shippagan gullies where there are now nothing but shoals. "Many indications," he wrote, "point to the conclusion that our shores are not in a condition of stability but are steadily sinking."

Unnoticed, or unremarked upon for several years, Ganong's observations on coastal subsidence surfaced as part of a heated, in physiographic terms, controversy. In articles in *Science* (in 1911) and the *Botanical Gazette* (in 1913), Douglas W. Johnson, a physiographer at Harvard, questioned the assumption of coastal subsidence based on botanical evidence. The year following, his colleague and principal ally James W. Goldthwait, in the article "Supposed Evidences of Subsidence of the Coast of New Brunswick in Modern Time," published by the Geological Survey of Canada in 1914, cited Ganong's article in the *Bulletin* as the offending source. While botanists and ecologists in general agreed with the assertion of coastal subsidence, as opposed to a rise in tide levels, only Ganong, according to Goldthwait, had said so in print. Inadvertently,

Ganong had questioned an article of faith. In 1899 William Morris Davis, a professor of physical geography, published his cycle of erosion theory purporting that landforms could be understood only if seen as a stage in a perpetual cycle of erosion. Davis's hypothesis rested on a sudden elevation of the land surface followed by uninterrupted eons of erosion. Barring interruptions of the cycle, landforms and the rivers flowing across them progressed from mountainous or elevated youth to peneplained old age. The theory, and the very successful text book, *Physical Geography*, that followed, salvaged Davis's faltering career at Harvard and promised to do the same for Johnson's. Johnson, whom Davis had taken under his wing at Harvard, had edited Davis's *Geographical Essays* (1909). Although not a gifted researcher, Johnson was an ardent acolyte and unswervingly partisan, attacking with equal zeal theories of coastal subsidence and, as a prominent member of the American Rights League, America's reluctance to engage Germany in the First World War. In Davisian circles, an hypothesis that proposed slow, more or less continuous vertical movement of the earth's crust, and downward movement in particular, was heresy.

In 1911 Johnson and Goldthwait visited the southern Gulf of St. Lawrence under the auspices of Harvard and the Geological Survey of Canada. Johnson went to the beach resort of Cascumpeque Harbour in Prince Edward Island and Goldthwait to the North Shore. Johnson found no evidence of subsidence in Prince Edward Island and concluded: "It may be noted…that the absence of anything approaching a continuous fringe of dead trees about Prince Edward Island is a very good indication that there has been no marked general subsidence in this region in recent times. There is, furthermore, good reason for believing that the whole Atlantic coastline…has enjoyed a period of approximate stability for several thousand years at least."

For his part in the debate, Goldthwait dismissed the evidence of drowned estuaries, underwater peat bogs, and submerged tree trunks as proving nothing for or against land levels. He also failed to see how Ganong's theory of barrier island formation could be connected with coastal subsidence. He argued that the barrier reefs had first formed offshore through the accumulation of shore drift between the headlands and were pushed slowly landward by waves, narrowing the intervening lagoons. When the islands reached the mainland the lagoons would vanish and the barrier reefs pass into true beach. A few months earlier, Johnson had pointed to a similar process in Prince Edward Island, the barrier reef at Richmond Bay being pushed ashore. In his book on shore processes and shoreline development, Johnson naturally welcomed Goldthwait's endorsement: "the laws of wave action" compelled abandonment of the subsidence theory.

Johnson's impressions of shore forms along the North Shore, based on Ganong's own fieldwork, supplemented by charts, and, as he conceded, "views from a passing train," pointed to fundamental differences in modes of inquiry. Ganong's was experiential: observe closely, discard preconceptions, and seek explanation. Observing closely meant paddling and poling in a one- or two-person, specially shod canoe and hauling measuring and mapping equipment along river and shore. Ganong, in Michael Caron's phrase, was a "particularist uninterested in establishing general or universal laws." For Johnson, on the other hand, actuality was chiefly a testing ground for proving, in this case, Davisian universals. Determined to deny or evade the evidence for subsidence, the Davisian physiographers, as the eminent geographer Carl Sauer remarked, set out to bag their own decoys.

By 1933, twenty years after the initial controversy, Goldthwait had suffered a change of mind and heart. In a letter to Ganong from Dartmouth College, he thanked Ganong for welcoming his son, Richard, when he was on a visit to Smith College, as he had long wanted him to make the acquaintance not only of one of the country's senior scientists but "one of the most distinguished, both in versatility and good sportsmanship." He thanked Ganong for a reprint of his earlier paper and continued:

> "I don't know whether Dick told you of the fun we are getting out of the Des Barres chart of Boston Harbor (1777) which shows the Nantasket shoreline very different from the present, and rather spoils Johnson's argument for coastal stability for the last 1,000–3,000 years. With your expert knowledge of old charts you'd find this case amusing, I'm sure. Maybe it's a sign of advancing age, but I find the borderland between

geologic time and modern historic time of increasing interest. And this problem of stability or subsidence in near-present time is interesting enough to call for study of every scrap of evidence. I hope you'll continue to dig up data bearing on it."

Ganong continued to dig. In a letter to the *Saint John Globe* on June 10, 1912, published immediately after Johnson and Goldthwait presented him with their pre-publication assertion that the coast of the North Shore was stable, Ganong, in addition to other items of evidence, alluded to maps: "In this connection I have worked over with care all of Champlain's detailed maps of harbors in comparison with the modern topography, and have found therein a good many additional facts implying a subsidence of the coast since his day." He found the maps and charts of harbours to be true sea charts designed to show mariners the safe entrances and good anchorages. In the charts drafted in 1605, areas explicitly marked as "bancs de sable" had long since been destroyed by the landward retreat of the beach. In the same article he pointed out that the head of tide on the Tabusintac was considerably above the levels shown on old plans. He had also been assured by residents of the Petitcodiac that the head of tide on that river had moved over a mile upstream in historic times. But his "best piece of evidence," soon to be published in the *Bulletin* of the NHSNB, was that the head of tide on the Main Southwest Miramichi in 1786 lay considerably below its present position at the mouth of the Renous and that the 1786 plan marks "Rapids" nearly half a mile below the Renous where now the tide flows without any break. He had not found any case showing movement of the head of tide down any of the rivers. Nor had he found evidence anywhere of the elevation of the coastline.

Unlike Goldthwait, Douglas Johnson held fast to his thesis of coastal stability, and like Goldthwait he bore Ganong no hard feelings. In 1923 he wrote to Ganong, expressing his pleasure that Ganong was contemplating a book on the physical geography of New Brunswick (it was never finished) and informing him that he would quote from his writings in a forthcoming book of his own. With Ganong's permission, he would also reproduce one or two of his illustrations even though he might disagree with Ganong's conclusions. He wrote:

To me, your work always seemed to have this special value, that whether or not one agreed with your conclusions, he could base himself with confidence on the facts [presented]. You keep your facts and theories separated, which unfortunately not all of us succeed in doing.... As regards differences of interpretation, I have always read your criticisms of my views with as much pleasure as I could any agreement with them because of the fairness with which you state the elements of the problem, and the gracious form in which you clothe your adverse views. I only hope I can succeed in making equally clear my appreciation of the value of your work and the fact that while I may differ with your opinions, I never differ with you.... I may take a trip along parts of the Acadian shoreline this summer, and if so, I will take the liberty of writing you again for suggestions as to places to see and how to get about. If you should be there at the same time, it would be delightful if we could get together.

Today the consensus of scientific opinion, and the weight of evidence, supports the view that the coastline is sinking. Alfred Redfield, the first modern scientist to estimate the onset and rate of coastal subsidence, in the late 1960s used Ganong's detailed studies of Champlain's harbour maps. Ganong was also convinced of a relationship between rates of coastline recession and rates of subsidence, pointing to the North Shore,

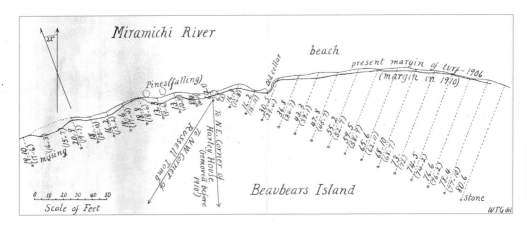

Ganong's measurements on the shore of Beaubears Island in the lower Miramichi to determine rates of coastal recession. New Brunswick Museum, Ganong Collection: F450-6

which is mostly low and little above sea level, where exposed unconsolidated glacial clays, sands, and soft organic materials were being washed away. However, he needed a measure of rates of recession. At the end of his 1904 field trip with Arthur Pierce he found, in a field on the north end of Beaubears Island, a line of old fence posts so positioned that measurements could be made at right angles from the fence line to the seaward edge of the eroding field. Beaubears Island is at the confluence of the Northwest and Southwest Miramichi rivers.

Six years later, on one of his last field trips with Pierce, he returned to Beaubears and with Pierce's help made a second set of measurements from each post to the shoreline. They were careful not to look at the old measurements until completing the new ones. They found that in the six year interval the coastline had receded by an average of more than half a metre. The north shore of Beaubears Island is sheltered so Ganong concluded that rates of recession would be greater on exposed ocean shores. To preserve the posts for future measurements, he protected them with boulders of cobblestone size gathered from the beach. And to preserve the centre of the decaying posts, he drove in a small pebble down to ground level. He counted on the measurements proving useful when someday (as did happen) a formula correlating rates of erosion and rates of subsidence had been worked out.

William Morris Davis, whose theory of an erosion cycle had fuelled the coastal subsidence debate, was not involved in it directly, but he would have known of Ganong. A decade earlier Henry C. Cowles, the eminent ecologist, had invited Ganong to be a founding member of the Association of American Geographers. Membership was conditional on original research and Cowles cited Ganong's raised peat bog and Bay of Fundy marsh studies. Ganong's co-sponsor was none other than W. M. Davis. Pleading society overload, Ganong declined the invitation: "I am very much obliged to you for the invitation to join the American Geographers Association, and am in full sympathy with its aims, but I belong to too many more things than I can be of any use to, thus I am obliged to decline."

Chapter 11

* දාළු ඉළ*

CRUCIAL MAPS

I used to know pretty well what was going on in their heads as they sat
before me, and we swayed like the branches of one tree; but now I see only
a set of masks, with no idea of what is going on behind them, and all
I can do is make the end of the affair as good as I can, and trust to luck
that they will manage to hook on somewhere. So I believe in the sixty-
eight year [retirement] rule and no exceptions; and am happy about
it because I can now complete some of the work for which the data are
abundantly in hand, but confusion has prevented completion of the form.
—W. F. Ganong

G anong retired from Smith in 1932. In a letter to Fannie Eckstorm, written the year previously, he confided that although he had not lost interest in teaching he had lost touch with his charges: a "great gulf" had opened between the students and himself. They were interested in the practice of life, he in its philosophy. It was the unbridge-able gap, as he put it, between those like himself with their heads in the clouds, and those with their feet on the ground.

The data abundantly in hand were materials for a series of monographs for the *Transactions of the Royal Society of Canada*, two of which were already completed, on the sixteenth-century cartography of eastern Canada and the south coast of Newfoundland, from Cape Race to Penobscot Bay. He told Eckstorm that he might regret the decision to complete the work, but the abundance of material represented years of painstaking and costly collection that he hated to see lost. In the days before the invention of easy and inexpensive copying and transmission, map reproductions and photographs, some of poor quality, had to be ordered and shipped. Many map collections had not been catalogued with the care that is now customary, and there was much confusion about authorship and dates. Free of teaching, Ganong could now complete the series. He expressed his relief to a fellow historian of cartography, friendly adversary, and long-time correspondent, G. R. F. Prowse. "But O! the luxury of not having to go at any fixed time to classes! The cartography goes on, however, I can always drop anything and turn to that with joy."

The result of this final effort was the monumental 470-page *Crucial Maps in the Early Cartography and Place-Nomenclature of the Atlantic Coast of Canada*. Completed in 1937, it was a compilation of nine monographs written for *Transactions* between 1929 and 1937, rounding off a publishing career in cartography that had begun in 1887 with his article on Cartier's first voyage and continued ten years later with his 1897 monograph on the mapping of New Brunswick.

Crucial maps, to speak biologically (Ganong's phrase), were maps that marked mutations or turning points in the cartography of eastern Canada. For this concluding work in cartography Ganong divided the Atlantic coast of Canada into three regions: the Greenland, Labrador, and Newfoundland coasts as far as Cape Race; Cape Race westward to the Cabot Strait, Cape Breton, Nova Scotia, and Maine to the Penobscot; and third, the Gulf of St. Lawrence. The mapping periods extend from the first voyage of John Cabot in 1497 down to the beginning of the seventeenth century; the second, "transitional" period began with Champlain's advanced maps of 1603 and continued until the beginning of the professional Admiralty surveys circa 1750.

The cartography of the period up to 1600 rested upon four official voyages of exploration: the English-sponsored voyages of John Cabot between 1497 and 1520; the voyages of the Portuguese Joam Alvares Fagundes between 1520 and 1530; the French-sponsored voyage of Jean de Verrazano 1524; and the Spanish voyage of Emilio Estevan Gomez in 1525. All were inspired by Columbus's initial voyage of 1492 that pointed to the western ocean as a possible route to the riches of the Orient. Most of the maps represented the efforts of sequestered geographers and map-makers at home to piece together the incomplete and often inconsistent data brought back by the explorers. Of well over a hundred maps drawn, only some half dozen (the crucial maps) were based on new discovery, the others being copies or combinations of parts of previously existing maps. Most of the original data was lost subsequently.

The Cabot voyages resulted in the famed Cosa map, completed shortly after 1500. Drawn and elaborately coloured on an oxhide surface one by one-and-a-half metres, it is the earliest known map to represent any part of North America. The western, transatlantic part of the map is shown on a larger scale than the Old World section. The map-maker, Juan de la Cosa, a Basque by birth long in the service of Spain and the owner and captain of Columbus's flagship the *Santa Maria*, was one of the greatest practical navigators and cartographers of his day. Most historians agree that his map, "rediscovered" by Alexander von Humboldt in 1832, is based upon a map made during the Cabot voyages. Which coast the map represents, however, has been a subject for debate. The candidates are the north coast of the Gulf of St. Lawrence, the south coast of Newfoundland, and the coast of Cape Breton Island. A further dilemma is whether the coast runs east–west, as shown, or north–south. Ganong attributed the east–west orientation to compasses corrected for the very different declination in Europe.

As for the coast depicted, Ganong opted for Cape Breton, arguing that Cabot missed Newfoundland on his outward voyage in 1497, made landfall on Cape Breton, and then returned along the south coast of Newfoundland. Ganong's exposition of the Cosa map, according to Theodore K. Layng, then head of the map division of the Public Archives of Canada and Honorary Librarian of the Royal Society of Canada, was one of the most brilliant ever written and his analysis of the Cabot voyages and the La Cosa map a masterpiece of inductive science. Ganong's chief adversary, G. R. F. Prowse of Winnipeg, argued for a Newfoundland landfall, insisting that the La Cosa map was a product of two English voyages, one in 1497 and the other in 1498, along the south coast of Newfoundland. Ganong's argument, however, had the support of most of the leading cartographers of the day and was endorsed by the Royal Society. The Society as such refrained from taking sides in the Cabot landfall debate, but in 1897 a committee of the society ruled that "the greatly preponderating weight of evidence" indicated the easternmost coast of Cape Breton Island as the most likely landfall.

Ganong's second monograph covered the years 1520–1530. In a series of maps, the Portuguese map-makers Lopo and Diego Homem drew the coastlines from Cape Race to Cape Breton and beyond. Their maps were based upon the voyages of Joam Alvares Fagundes who explored under the official authorization of the King of Portugal. As hope of finding a northern passage to the Orient dimmed, Fagundes in later voyages attempted settlement, leaving a score of place names of evident Portuguese origin on the coast of Cape Breton. About half of these have survived. Other novel features of the Homem maps are the introduction of the Bay of Fundy and, on the east coast of Cape Breton Island, Mi'kmaq place names. These are the oldest Aboriginal names known to Europeans in Canada. Some of them are were noted in Silas Rand's dictionary as well as in manuscript lists generously supplied to Ganong by Father Pacifique. According to Layng, Ganong's analysis of the cartographic origins of the Bay of Fundy and his dissertation on place names will remain a classic.

The third monograph dealt with the maps of Visconte Maggiolo, 1527, and Henry de Verrazzano, 1529, inspired by the voyage of Jean (Giovanni) da Verrazzano along the Atlantic coast in 1524. Henry and Jean da Verrazzano were brothers. South of the Bay of Fundy, the east coast of the continent was uncharted. Spaniards had mapped the coast of Florida, but until Verrazzano's voyage the coast from Florida northward had to be filled with ocean or a coast that was obviously imaginary. Under the auspices of King Francis I of France, Jean da Verrazzano sailed from Dieppe in 1524 in search of a passage along the uncharted east coast to the East Indies and China. He took the Columbus route, reaching North America south of Cape Fer in North Carolina. He then followed the coast north to Cape Cod and Cape Breton, and then sailed hurriedly to Newfoundland before returning to France. Verrazzano's original report and map were lost, but Italian forms of his letter, summarizing the out-standing features of the voyage to the King, have survived. Maggiolo's and Henry da Verrazzano's maps match the Letter so closely that their source could only have been Jean da Verrazzano's lost map. The only critical study of Verrazzano's expedition to follow Ganong's before the 1964 publication of *Crucial Maps*—Dr. Bernard Hoffmann's *From Cabot to Cartier* (1961)—fully accepted Ganong's reconstruction.

The maps of Diego Ribero and Alonso de Chavez, the subject of the fourth monograph, were based on the voyages of Estevan Gomez in 1525. A native of Portugal, Gomez was one of the most eminent and experienced navigators in the service of Spain. Sent by King Charles to find a passage to the Orient, he sailed in a caravel from Corunna in September 1524 to search for a passage between Florida and the Bacalaos—the Spanish name for the combined Newfoundland–Cape Breton region—and returned in August 1525. From Spain he sailed to Cuba and Florida, and then up the east coast as far as New England, and possibly, according to Ganong, into the Bay of Fundy as far as the mouth of the St. John River, and then back to Corunna. No report of the voyage has survived, but the results of it are strongly embodied in world maps made by the best cartographers of the time. Subsequent research may have overturned some of the details, but Theodore Layng regarded Ganong's analysis of the records and maps as a "truly remarkable" study.

The last of the official voyages in the period planned initially for the series (1497–1527) was that of John Rut. Directed by Henry VIII to find a northwestern or polar passage to Asia, two ships left Bristol in June 1527. The vessels entered the Davis Strait but were trapped by ice. Rut's vessel escaped, but the other disappeared. Rut set his passage for Newfoundland, "Cape Britton," and the coast of New England where he was to search for the legendary settlement of Norumbega. On his return to England in the late autumn, possibly via the West Indies, he would have submitted a report, but it did not survive; nor is the effect of the voyage traceable upon any map.

Cartier's epic voyages that followed (1534–1542), to the Gulf of St. Lawrence and down the St. Lawrence River, Ganong had already described in a much earlier TRSC report, and because they hardly affected the mapping of the outer coast of Canada his first thought was to omit them. However, the four hundredth anniversary of the first Cartier voyage (1534) happened to fall within the period envisaged by the series, and in the interim H. P. Biggar, the London representative of the Public Archives of Canada, had published (in 1924) an outstanding account of the voyages. Ganong considered it the most comprehensive and critical work of the Cartier voyages yet attempted. For both of these reasons, Ganong felt he had to include them.

Under patent from King Francis I of France, Cartier made three voyages, the first two of epic proportions. His instructions, reflecting the new motive for exploration, had been "to explore and take possession of New France" and to look for the elusive north passage to Cathay where he might find islands and countries rich in gold. He found neither passage nor gold, but by exploring the gulf and the river (1535–1536), he opened the door to a continent. The great southern or Cabot Strait entrance to the gulf appeared to have been missed (disputed by G. R. F. Prowse, who contended the English had beaten the French to it) by earlier voyagers. John Cabot might have seen it and mistaken it for an enclosed bay. Fagundes, who was a colonizer rather than a searcher, might also have explored it in 1527 but recorded it on maps so greatly minimized (possibly to exclude competitors) that subsequent maps closed it altogether. Verrazzano, thinking the region sufficiently explored, ignored it, passing directly from Cape Breton to Newfoundland. Gomez was never near it.

Although Cartier's original records were lost, condensed summaries of them and contemporary compilations from his maps survived. Even if not written or drawn by him, these, according to Ganong, rank with the great commentaries of history. They gave Canada its first classics, and because of them it has been possible to work out Cartier's geography and cartography much more fully than those of his predecessors on the Atlantic coast. According to Theodore Layng, Ganong's and Biggar's masterly critiques, and the main points of their reconstructions, are not likely to be seriously challenged. The historian Ramsay Cook considered Ganong's *Crucial Maps* to be still the standard work on Cartier's discoveries, and in his review of the early monographs in the series G. M. Wrigley, editor of the *Geographical Review*, the journal of the

American Geographical Society, described Ganong as "a master of his material." In a letter to Ganong in 1935 Louis Karpinski of the University of Michigan considered Ganong's method—"detailed study of a given region, with the maps before you, and detailed study of the place names as well as delineations"—to be the only way in which real progress in cartographical studies could be made. "Your studies help to place the various MSS maps in their proper places and I have found great profit in that side of your work."

Ganong as a cartologist, a student of maps, had no greater admirer than Dr. Lawrence Wroth, librarian of the John Carter Brown Library, research professor of American history at Brown, and author of *The Voyages of Giovanni da Verrazzano* (1970):

> Ganong's Crucial Maps *has been a source of information, instruction, and inspiration to me for a great many years. Quite aside from the integrity and fairness of the work itself I know of no other book in historical cartography in which intensity of purpose, scholarly method, and first-hand observation have come so happily together. His chapters on Cabot and Verrazzano have been in my hands as a chief reliance throughout the years of my work on Verrazzano. I have never questioned that the desire to make a statement as nearly perfect as might be underlay all his effort. It has been a satisfaction to me to realize that year by year his work has become better known, and his conclusions have won wider acceptance.*

Dr. Lawrence Martin, head of the map division of the Library of Congress, was of like mind. He and his colleagues were in awe of the ways in which Ganong had worked out so brilliantly the sources of successive maps from an original type. Martin considered the compiled monographs that constitute *Crucial Maps* to be "one of the most important contributions in this field which has ever been published in America."

Of the post-Cartier monographs in the series, the most important dealt with Mercator's 1569 world chart, part of which shows the Atlantic coast. No new voyages of exploration had followed Cartier's so the chart's merit rested not in the presentation of new data but in the introduction of a method of assembling and evaluating existing data and presenting the conclusions in, as Ganong phrased it, "stark unadorned realism." Tied to existing sources, Mercator's efforts to supplant subjective idealism with unadorned realism were only partly successful. Even so, his map was a watershed that separated the old from the new cartography. Working with scant, incomplete data and required to produce pleasing maps or pictures, cartographers in Europe were engaged less in a study of sober geography than in the perpetuation of cartographical error. Ganong regarded the matching of old maps against new to be a pointless exercise. The former can be understood only in the light of their evolution and under the limitations and conventions of their time.

Although Mercator had no better data than his predecessors, his chart is qualitatively different. From existing manuscripts and charts, he selected the most reliable information and subjected his compilation to the demands of a new method of projection. Whereas old maps were drawn to magnetic or special compass meridians, the new projection required adjustment to true meridians and parallels that entailed a corresponding well-known enlargement of the land northward that was readily comprehended by seamen. Mercator's chart was a mutation in cartographical method rather than geographical knowledge. Ganong described it as the first chart of the region drawn with realistic intent, freed from artistic and other conventions and from ulterior motives. As such it was, in principle, the first venture toward a scientific cartography for Canada. It remained for Champlain to take the next crucial step: the search for original geographic data through personal exploration.

GANONG AND G. R. F. PROWSE

Outside the academy, Ganong's closest associate in cartology, as well as his chief adversary, was G. R. F. Prowse of Winnipeg. Their association began in 1897 when Ganong wrote to Prowse, then at Aachen in the Rhineland, to ask how he might obtain copies of maps in the *History of Newfoundland,* a book written by Prowse's father, Judge D. W. Prowse. George Prowse, the son, had done much of the cartological work for his father's book. A stickler for correct usage, Prowse pointed out (in a correction Ganong endorsed) that cartography, the commonly used

G. R. F. Prowse, 1937. New Brunswick Museum: 1987-17-482

word, referred to the making of maps, and cartology to the study of them. Prowse had been educated at Haileybury College in England, the mother country, Newfoundland then being a colony. After Haileybury, where he studied chemistry, he worked in the dyeing and textile business, first in Yorkshire (at his family's firm) then variously in Germany, New England, and Philadelphia, all the while pursuing at libraries and museums in London, Paris, and Boston the exploration and mapping of Canada's Atlantic coast. In 1904 he presented a paper, subsequently printed, on Cabot's landfall at the Eighth International Geographic Congress in New York. He planned to visit Ganong after the conference but instead had to take an ailing sister to England for medical treatment and resign his position in Philadelphia. The following year he moved to Manitoba, where he joined two brothers, and took up school teaching from which he retired in 1925.

In 1897, when he was working on his monograph on the cartography of New Brunswick for the TRSC, Ganong approached Prowse, as some of the maps in the elder Prowse's book seemed applicable to Ganong's study. The correspondence continued until a year or two before Ganong's death in 1941. The two men never met. One early result of their correspondence was Ganong's decision to confine his first studies to the coast of New Brunswick and not pursue the cartography of the Gulf of St. Lawrence. The wealth of material on the gulf collected by Prowse was much greater than his own. Later, about 1930, Ganong referred again to the extent of the Prowse collection: "These materials you so generously entrust to me have rather stunned me.... Even in the NB–NS territory, which I thought I knew pretty well as to map literature, you have many things new to me, and in cases material that I would have been most sorry to miss. Anyhow, it knocked a lot of conceit out of me, and, incidentally, sent your knowledge still higher in my estimation."

Their exchanges were occasional at first but became frequent after Prowse's retirement and Ganong's championing of a Cabot landfall on Cape Breton in his 1929 monograph for *Transactions*. Prowse was just as adamant about a landfall at Bonavista, on the south coast of Newfoundland. It was the subject of a heated, but amicable, decade-long debate. As a schoolteacher in Manitoba, Prowse had no institutional backing, and aside from published articles the bulk of his work is available only in mimeographed form; it is extremely scarce and seldom quoted. Nevertheless, according to Theodore Layng, it is an amazing reference source for anyone interested in the exploration and mapping of Canada's Atlantic coast. Prowse's *Cartological Material,* which he completed in 1936 and had worked on since 1894, may have been the first systematic effort to trace early discoveries along Canada's northeast coastline using cartographic evidence. In spite of his preoccupation with Cabot, Prowse's declared objective had been to trace fifteen primary surveys of the whole northeast coast, from Baffin Island to Maine.

Ganong and Prowse traded information and insults in equal measure, Prowse in one sentence congratulating Ganong for the great reasonableness of his letters over thirty-five years and in the next dismissing his views in a recent essay on Portuguese exploration. Ganong never took offence: "It's all ok—all's fair in love, war, and cartography." Prowse contended that the Atlantic coast of Canada and the St. Lawrence were discovered, surveyed, and mapped by early English navigators, the Portuguese, and French arriving later chiefly as colonizers guided by English maps. Aside from Ganong's and Prowse's deep interests in the mapping of the Atlantic coast, the heat of their exchanges owed much to the licence for speculation granted by thin and often inconclusive evidence. "We cartologists," Prowse wrote in 1909, "beat the metaphysicians hands down in being able from the same data of reality in the <u>most</u> disinterested way to arrive at such diverse conclusions." The heatedness was also stoked by the sheer difficulty of the work. Once reached, conclusions were difficult to give up. "Our work is both hard to write and hard to read, even for specialists," wrote Prowse; and "Every map you send me has something new and important. This is no mere soft solder, but the very perplexing fact that makes our work so difficult, so fascinating and opens up many problems undreamt of still in our philosophy." Ganong, apologizing for earlier misunderstandings, countered with "It's a hard job to present these evasive matters clearly, no matter how definite they may be in one's own mind."

Ganong was equally admiring of Prowse, and bowed to Prowse's greater knowledge of parts of the field. He also leaned heavily on the many cartographic items Prowse sent him. In 1933 Ganong wrote,

"You'd think I was the master and you the pupil wouldn't you? But it's the other way round, only like most pupils I think it is the master not I is the one who is 'verruckt'! [deranged]" and "your letters, even if I cannot answer them at once, are among the most welcoming and stimulating that I receive, and are very carefully read and re-read." Only his diverse interests prevented immediate replies.

But mutual admiration did not still their rivalry nor restrain their pens. In some ways it was a case of the cautious, disciplined, and established academic versus the gifted (but sometimes impatient and occasionally reckless) outsider. Ganong was undisguisedly critical of Prowse's stretching of the facts to justify his position on the Cabot landing and his use of a "quasi-cabalistic" system of numbered letter symbols that overwhelmed the reader and left him impatient and irritated: "I have read this through three or four times in my efforts to understand it. Your letter symbols act like grains of sand when trying to eat good cooked food—a great annoyance. If you keep this system your work will never be used, and no cartologist will make any serious attempt to follow it." In their early exchanges, he also chided Prowse for not distinguishing clearly between accepted fact and unsubstantiated theories of his own. A counter-argument, for non-specialist readers in particular, had to be built slowly and systematically from a firm foundation. Guerilla attacks from the flanks were not convincing. But for Prowse's "microscopic method" (that seems to have closely resembled his own) for analyzing place names in Newfoundland and Labrador he had nothing but praise. Ganong also admired Prowse's spirited, maverick temper, writing in 1930: "Hope all goes well with you, including some conversion to the true faith of Ganong, Biggar, and other pontiffs but it is darned good for us to have a rebel like you." Also: "It's a delight to have a shining mark to shoot at, and I can continue to contest your ideas in the assurance that you are the serene student to whom good evidence will finally appeal. [...] Nothing can disturb our friendly personal relations."

For his part, Ganong relished Prowse's frank and obviously friendly criticism of his own work. "When I see 'rubbish' in the margin of a paper returned from Prowse I get an extra thrill and grin." In a 1933 letter to Prowse on the eve of the submission of his article on the Cartier voyages, claiming primacy for the French in the discovery of the Gulf of St.

Lawrence, Ganong quipped that it would allow Prowse, in favour of an earlier English discovery, "to open up his artillery again." Yet three years later Ganong disapproved of the naming of the Cabot trail in Cape Breton as affirmation of the Cabot landfall. However strong Ganong's conviction, and the strength of the collective support, the point was not proven. The same reservation applied to the naming of the Cabot Strait, as this too amounted to what he called loading the evidence in the public mind.

Toward the end of their correspondence, and their lives, Ganong and Prowse were friends, their exchanges warmer and not confined to cartology. The most interesting digression was Ganong's response to an inquiry from Prowse about the late President Coolidge. Coolidge died in 1933, and his obituary notices would have referred to his years in Northampton. He practised law in the city from 1898 to 1906, served as a city councillor, and returned to Northampton after the presidency. Ganong replied that he knew him well. Early in their careers, he and Coolidge had been near neighbours on Massasoit Street and in the mornings frequently walked downtown together to their respective workplaces, Coolidge to his law office and Ganong to Smith. Ganong admired him, belying Coolidge's reputation for coolness and calculation. He wrote:

> I greatly liked and respected him and now have a real reverence for his memory. He was a man great in ability, honesty, sense of duty and restraint, and one whom clamour could not budge. The great American public estimated him correctly and only the "intelligentsia" had him wrong—and in my opinion his life was a great service to the American people....I always thought his weakest point was his foreign policy—he did not understand Europe, which he had never seen, judging the nations there too much by the standards of this country, in its impregnable security. But in the [matters] of human character which endure despite the fluctuations of political history, and those which carry mankind forward in the long run, he was a very great man.... The more intimately people knew him, the more they admired and respected him—and he has long been a greatly beloved figure in this region that knew him best. He was the exception in that he was a prophet most highly honoured in his own country. This is my opinion of him.

By 1933, the Ganong–Prowse salutations had moved, if not quite to first names, then to affectionate alternatives: "My Dear Ganong," or "My Dear Friend Prowse," and penultimately from Ganong, "My Great and Good Brother," and "My Great and Good Friend." Prowse in 1939 rose to signing off, "Yrs affectionately." After Ganong's death, he wrote affectingly to Anna to say that Ganong had been like a brother to him. Anna replied in kind, telling Prowse that a perennial delight had been the arrival of his letters with postscripts spilling out the sides.

Just as telling as any written avowal of loyalty or affection was Prowse's decision to donate his map and document collection to the New Brunswick Museum in Saint John. In December 1939, Prowse wrote to Dr. Murray MacLaren, president of the museum, that he wished to leave, as a gift to the museum, his research material on the discovery and exploration of the northeast Atlantic coast that he had amassed since 1894. He had considered offering the collection to the British Museum in London, or the John Carter Brown Library in Providence, Rhode Island, but on hearing that Ganong, with whom he had been working intimately since 1929, intended leaving his collection to the NBM, he felt he should do likewise. Their combined documents and maps would make the most complete special collection of the coast from Greenland to Maine.

From Dr. J. C. Webster, who had been a prime mover in founding the museum, Prowse learned that his maps and documents would be housed in a special research room—an alcove on the top floor overlooking the St. John River—being set aside for the Ganong collection. When Ganong was dying, Webster told him that his and Prowse's map and document collections would occupy the same space; Ganong smiled and said: "That will be fine."

Chapter 12

———————— ᎒ᎧᏋ ᎩᏋᎧ ————————

J. C. WEBSTER AND
THE NEW BRUNSWICK
MUSEUM

In the 1920s, in his last years of teaching, Ganong met his doppel-gänger. Physically, he and John Clarence Webster were not unalike: both were of slight build, both tireless researchers and scholars, and in their ambitions for New Brunswick they were near brothers. They were born within a year of each other (Webster at Shediac in 1863), and they had curiously similar career paths. Webster had been a renowned physician and surgeon who, in his late fifties, gave up medicine to devote himself to the history and culture of New Brunswick and the Maritimes. Ganong's trajectory had been similar, but less precipitate. He continued to teach and run a very successful botany department until his retirement, but his research interests lay elsewhere. In a world as small as New Brunswick their paths were bound to cross.

Webster graduated from Mount Allison University when he was only sixteen and from there, he went to Edinburgh, Scotland, where he studied medicine and where he might have settled had a dank, wet climate and successive attacks of laryngitis and bronchitis not threatened to permanently damage his health. He specialized in obstetrics and gynecology in

Leipzig and Berlin as well as Edinburgh, conducted research, and wrote medical texts translated into several languages that were used worldwide. On his return to Canada in 1896, Webster taught at McGill and practised at the Royal Victoria Hospital. His final professional move, three years later, was to Chicago, Illinois, as Professor of Obstetrics and Gynecology at the Rush Medical College, an affiliate of the University of Chicago. He remained there until 1920, conducting an extensive and lucrative private practice while revolutionizing the teaching of gynecology and obstetrics. At age fifty-seven, Webster retired to Shediac to immerse himself in Maritime and eastern Canadian culture and history. His colleagues and the college thought him mad, the latter deciding not to replace him for a year on the assumption he would return. He didn't go back nor did he, as they had predicted, die of ennui. New Brunswick and the Maritimes were also his country. He quipped that at school and Mount Allison he was well enough grounded in English history, but for all he learned of New Brunswick and Maritime history he might as well have gone to school in Patagonia.

In spite of the strength of Ganong's and Webster's mutual interests, arranging a meeting proved difficult. Ganong was in no hurry to meet him. Summer was the most convenient time since the pair were both in New Brunswick, but Ganong's summers, no matter how pressing the social and professional obligations, belonged to the rivers and the woods. He declined Webster's first invitation to Shediac in 1921, apologizing on his return to Northampton: "I made a poor return to your very kind invitation this summer, but in the vacation I am a sort of back to nature vagabond, immensely interested in wandering about and seeing places and objects of interest in N.B. and not a bit inclined to don the garments and customs of civilized society. My relatives in N.B. of whom I have a host, find me quite hopeless in this respect, though my intentions and promises are always good!" In a subsequent letter, he was even more forthcoming: "It is a great satisfaction to know that there is now in New Brunswick an interested student of these matters so competent as yourself, and I hope for a closer acquaintance in the future." The hope, however, did not materialize as a visit to Shediac. The following summer Ganong repeated the refrain: "There is no explanation or excuse for my failure to appear

John Clarence Webster in his library. New Brunswick Museum: 1987-17-474

except that my word about visiting, especially in summer, is quite worthless, as you see. I don't care much about visiting anyhow, and in summer I am [so] absorbed in vagabonding about with canoe, car or tent, living freely and independently out of doors…that I find it quite impossible to turn civilized, and dress up, and be a visitor."

For Webster, who was urbane and patrician, a meeting in the New Brunswick woods was also quite impossible. He shared many interests with Ganong, but vagabonding and chumming with woodsmen, Aboriginals, and fishermen was not among them. If they were to meet it would be in winter in Northampton. But even this was not straightforward. In early December 1921, Webster wrote from Chicago and New York offering to travel by train to Northampton if they could agree upon a day and time. A Tuesday afternoon would be most convenient for him, but on Tuesdays Ganong had a class that he could not cancel nor leave to a colleague. He would be free on the following day but that did not suit Webster. However, they did manage a meeting—on which day is not clear—lunching at Ganong's house on Prospect Heights, a short walk from Smith. Webster took a cab from the station. The meeting was a success: "a pleasure of the first order," wrote Ganong, and he "rejoiced" that New Brunswick was fortunate enough to have a man of Webster's great knowledge, judgement, and energy, and said that he would consider it a privilege to support his efforts to advance affairs in the province. The particular advance Webster had in mind, and which they had evidently discussed, was a cultural centre for Saint John that would serve the sciences, literature, and the arts.

By the following September (1922) the focus had narrowed. The Dominion archivist, Arthur G. Doughty, informed Webster of the Archives's interest in setting up a provincial branch in Saint John and presumably one in each of the other Maritime provinces. Ganong was enthused, telling Webster that the need was urgent in light of the moribund state of the Historical Society. Interest had waned and members were dying. For Ganong, the idea of an archives and a museum for Saint John had been hatching for years. In Germany, he had seen the public value of museums, and a few years after his return he wrote for the newly founded *Acadiensis* an article named "On the Use and Value of

Historical Museums" (1902). He regarded museums not simply "as an accompaniment of an advancing civilization...[but] also, in a certain way, a measure of it. Where, he asked, was New Brunswick's historical museum, adding that it must astonish people of culture who visit Saint John to learn there is no such place. The province might be young, but it had a varied and interesting past. Loyalist and other artifacts were scattered throughout and, unless collected, they would soon be lost. As a home for them, Ganong suggested the old Ward Chipman house, in his opinion, the most interesting historical building in the city. Although not fireproof, it could (to some extent) be fireproofed with slow-burning floors and fireproof doors. As for funds, he asserted there might be a number of potential donors and both the city—which would benefit from an increase in tourist traffic—and the province could maintain it.

For an archives or a museum, fireproofing is critical. Thirty years after writing the article, Ganong told Webster if the new building proposed by the Dominion Archives were fireproofed and managed by Archives staff, he would probably be willing to leave his entire collection to it. He regarded his collection of New Brunswick books and documents as unrivalled, and they would be a nucleus for the museum library. Two weeks later, in a letter to Webster, Ganong repeated his desire to have a provincial home for his collection. If, on retirement, he should settle in or near Saint John, then he would help to support it but not, as Webster had hoped, as director.

Ganong deplored the loss of local and regional material to Ottawa, contending that each province should have its own archives. Webster, too, vehemently opposed the losses, writing of "the looting and denudation of the Provinces...for the benefit of Ottawa." Relations between W. C. Milner, the Dominion Archives Maritime representative in Saint John, and the city and provincial governments were not always cordial. Arthur G. Doughty had begged Webster to bequeath his collection to the Dominion Archives, but Webster balked, insisting he would do so only if it set up a branch in New Brunswick. The reward for the Dominion Archives would be Webster's collection of material on the Seven Years' War in Canada.

In a letter to Ganong later that month, on October 30, 1922, Webster indicated that government interest, in view of costs, had shifted to the idea of one central institution for the Maritimes, possibly located in Moncton.

The obvious frontrunners were Saint John or Halifax, but Moncton geographically was more central and would be particularly convenient for residents of PEI. If chosen, it would also, as Webster indicated, reduce occasions for friction between Saint John and Halifax. Moncton, he added presciently, was growing and had cultural and commercial ambitions, offering itself as a possible location for a proposed united group of colleges. Webster was loudly critical of Maritime tendencies to parochialism, reviling, as a proponent of federated universities, Mount Allison's decision to withdraw, against the wishes of the regents, from a proposed federation with Dalhousie and King's College in Nova Scotia. Ganong, who was more attuned to Maritime sentiments, questioned the proposal of a single archives on grounds that it would not capitalize on provincial loyalties. A centralized Maritime institution would be preferable to the current Ottawa-dominated arrangement, but it would only be a halfway measure. Although central and growing, he did not think Moncton, still essentially a railway node and repair centre, was quite ready for such an institution. The only satisfactory solution to the problem of the drain of material was a building in each province. It wouldn't allay all jealousies as there would still be what he called the "Fredericton–Saint John feeling," but that was relatively slight and most people of good sense would recognize Saint John's stronger claim.

Ganong's own loyalties and historical interests were so provincial that he admitted to Webster he couldn't conceive of leaving his collection to a centralized Maritime institution, even one based in Moncton. Webster he regarded as more worldly and cosmopolitan than he, and Webster's collection, made up of paintings, artifacts, books, and documents, was of much wider scope than his own. Webster's prime interests were the British general James Wolfe and the Seven Years' War, followed by the history of Acadia and the Maritimes. Furthermore, his wife, Alice Lusk Webster, was a collector and connoisseur of oriental and European art. In his reply to Ganong's letter that opted for a Saint John location, Webster wrote, in January 1923, that he had spoken to city officials and prominent citizens in Saint John about Ottawa's idea of a branch archives and suggested to them that a joint city/provincial cultural centre might appeal to Ottawa.

Pastel portrait of Ganong by Kathleen Shackleton completed in 1943. Kathleen was the sister of Sir Ernest Shackleton, the Antarctic explorer. NEW BRUNSWICK MUSEUM, GANONG COLLECTION: 1944-562 (1)

Webster's historical interests, like Ganong's, also extended to actual locations: of significant buildings, forts, landing places, skirmishes, treaty signings, and the need for their physical commemoration. In 1923 Webster had been appointed provincial representative to the Historic Sites and Monuments Commission of Canada, and much of Webster and Ganong's correspondence related to the wording of inscriptions and the placing of markers. In an October 1924 letter to Webster, acknowledging Webster's appointment, Ganong resolved to give his entire attention to New Brunswick matters. He believed, as did Webster, that for most people, material links with the past—either in the form of exact locations or surviving structures—were crucial to their shared sense of history.

As an aide Ganong was enthusiastic, balking only when it was suggested that certain marker monuments be placed at some distance from the places and incidents they were intended to mark: "It seems to me they wholly lose their point when this is done, and the sentiment is emptied all out of the matter. There is something moving and impressive—probably something of the animism surviving in our savage ancestry, some belief that the persons, scenes, or events survive there yet in spirit—in standing on the spot, or close enough to be an actual human witness where some great event has occurred, but this seems to me all lost when you read an inscription which tells you that [the incident or event occurred] somewhere else." To some, a little distance from the actual location did not matter, but as his exasperated colleague Arthur Pierce remarked at Ganong's obsessive fixing of the exact locations of seemingly insignificant and sometimes fleeting topographical features, it mattered to him.

After a hiatus, the museum issue surfaced again in 1927. In a letter to Webster dated July 15, 1927, Ganong noted a change he had made to his will before leaving Northampton: he had bequeathed his entire collection to the Public Archives in Ottawa with the proviso that if it should build a branch in New Brunswick, the collection should be moved there. Earlier that year, A. S. Doughty had written to Ganong describing the proposed new building for the Dominion Archives in Ottawa (and sending a sketch) in an effort to entice Ganong to leave his collection in his hands. Before writing to Webster, Ganong had just returned from a visit to the Crown Land Office in Fredericton where he'd heard of a well-backed movement in Fredericton to build a provincial museum and archives that would combine the holdings of the legislature and the university. In spite of his preference for Saint John, Ganong conceded that the seat of the legislature and the university might be the right place for it after all.

In his reply to Ganong, Webster indicated there were similar stirrings in Saint John. Dr. Murray MacLaren—physician, federal member of parliament for Saint John–Albert, prospective lieutenant-governor, and a strong supporter of the sciences and the arts—had told Webster he might have access to funds through a benefactor to build a provincial museum. MacLaren also had funds of his own that he was prepared to use, and did. The museum would combine the collections of the NHSNB and the Historical Society. If built, fireproofed, and professionally run, MacLaren wondered if Ganong would hold to his earlier promise of entrusting his collection it. Premier John Baxter, who was in favour of a Saint John location, appointed a committee to report on the relative merits of Saint John and Fredericton and insisted that Webster be the chair. Webster continued to resist Doughty's blandishments from Ottawa and let it be known that he, like Ganong, would consider leaving his collection only to a fireproof, professionally run museum in Saint John. The NHSNB was also adamant that its collection remain in the city. Webster indicated that to counter determined opposition from Fredericton—the issue had become political—a written assurance from Ganong might be pivotal. So, too, Webster added, might an offer from Ganong to serve as director on his retirement from Smith.

Ganong, however, already at work on the cartography of the North Atlantic and, determined to resist offerings of official or public positions on his return to New Brunswick, had other plans. "Freedom," he wrote to Webster in 1931, "is what I crave." He agreed to serve on the museum's executive committee but declined the directorship on the grounds that it would have been far too demanding. Unwilling to let his collection be a pawn in a tussle between Saint John and Fredericton, he suggested to Webster that to resolve the issue Fredericton might have the Archives and Saint John everything else: his own and Webster's collections as well as the collections of NHSNB and the Historical Society. The Saint John faction in the premier's Webster-chaired committee prevailed, and in 1930 building began in Saint John. The committee had hoped for a city centre location, but land costs and the generally hard times prevented this. The site eventually chosen, on an avenue of fine houses overlooking the harbour and backing onto the mighty St. John River, might not have been central, but it was commanding. So too was the building's Palladian facade.

The museum opened in August 1934, the 150th anniversary of the founding of the province, under the directorship of William Mackintosh, an entomologist, naturalist, and curator of the NHSNB museum (1898–1932). In spite of his professed dislike of grand public occasions, Ganong attended with his family and in a letter to Prowse in Winnipeg, admitted that he thoroughly enjoyed the occasion: two days of speech-making,

The New Brunswick Museum in Saint John, 1930. New Brunswick Museum: XI 1448

military parades, marching bands, concerts, and a ball. Three years later he was re-elected to the executive committee for three more years and, on a motion brought forward by Clarence Webster, Ganong was appointed Honorary Archivist of the museum.

Chapter 13

LAST DAYS

In November 1937, in a letter to Fannie Eckstorm, Ganong referred to his faltering health: "You will note a difficult handwriting, which I hope you can read. One little impediment time has brought me is stiffening fingers—no [help] for it except that they cannot with a pen keep up with my thoughts—and despite every effort I have never been able to compose on a typewriter." A year later, when she saw him in Northampton at her fiftieth Smith reunion, he was frail and handicapped, his voice weak. Parkinson's disease (paralysis agitans) had impaired his speech and made control of his hands difficult. Ganong had never managed the hoped-for move to Saint John. At the time of his retirement in 1932, the Great Depression was so deep that he could not, as he told Webster, have given his house away, and by the late thirties his two children were settled in Northampton schools. He had to remind himself continually, as he also told Webster, that three-fourths of his family were American. Through the thirties, too, his share of the income from the family business had shrunk; not to the point of penury, but enough that he had considered delaying his retirement.

He did not stop working. Volume nine of *Crucial Maps* was in the hands of the printers, and the series was still not finished. He wrote Eckstorm: "I thought there would only be one more, but there have to be two—but not very long, and the work is all done except for the final writing." He had begun work on volume ten, on Champlain, but had not written much, although, as Anna told Webster, there were many notes. First Nations nomenclature was now his most absorbing interest. To Eckstorm in 1937 he wrote, "Well, the Indian place name [study] goes rather well notwithstanding. It is my greatest interest—and hard to resist the temptation and drop everything else for it—but things keep crowding in that cannot be avoided." Although he had the data for most of the names entered on sheets, none had been written in the final form. His objective was an Aboriginal place-name study of the entire Maritimes. To Professor Gates, who had written in April 1937 for a list of his writings on Aboriginal place nomenclature, he replied, "It may be appropriate to add that I am now at work on a monograph of the entire subject (Indian Place Nomenclature of the Maritime Provinces) but it will be some time yet before it is completed. It is my chief hobby now that I am retired from active Emeritus work." Although never finished, Fannie Eckstorm would describe it as the most important collection of material on Aboriginal names that had yet been gathered.

When he arrived in Rothesay in the summer of 1941, Ganong could not speak. Even whispers, as Webster wrote to Prowse, had become mere lip movements. In late August he was moved from his sister's summer cottage to her house in Rothesay and in early September to Saint John General Hospital where he died ten days later. He was seventy-seven.

In a letter to Webster on the subject of his burial, Anna Ganong specified that his gravestone should be inconspicuous, a marker only, and of New Brunswick stone. Webster suggested Charlotte County granite. For an inscription Anna wondered if the maxim, or some variation thereof, Ganong had adopted from the title page of Peter Fisher's *History of New Brunswick*, "Whatever touches my country, interests me; I follow nature with truth my guide," might be too secular. Evidently it was, or was regarded as unsuitable for other reasons, because it is not on the stone. The funeral service was held at Ganong's brother Arthur's house in St. Stephen followed by burial in the St. Stephen Rural Cemetery attended by family and friends, Clarence Webster among them. By request, there were no flowers.

The final observance was at Smith. As a devotee of the college, and the first college marshall, Ganong would have approved. He wrote his own tribute to the college in response to an article Anne Seelye, President Seelye's daughter-in-law, had written for the *Alumnae Quarterly* at the time of his retirement. She explained how Ganong's "genius" as a teacher coupled with his profound modesty had opened the door to "the high adventure of learning." Ganong responded: "It has always been a deep satisfaction to serve Smith College, partly because of the fine spirit of intellectual freedom which President Seelye inculcated so successfully and partly because one's efforts seemed always to win full appreciation. I would not choose differently had I the power to choose again in the light of all I now know." Just before his retirement he told Webster he would always cherish Smith for granting him the freedom and support to pursue anything he wanted to do.

The Smith ceremony, held in early May 1942, was a tree-planting late one afternoon attended by a small group of friends at College Lane on the slope overlooking the Plant House and Paradise Pond. Mr. McLeod, the campus tree surgeon, had asked if he could plant a Canadian sugar maple in Ganong's honour. A hole was dug, the sapling held in place, and the hole filled. Ganong's daughter, Ann, threw in the last spadeful of soil.

Following Ganong's death, tributes arrived in number. Webster had solicited several for memorial occasions he had planned, and others arrived from colleagues, admirers, and former students. Fannie Eckstorm wrote simply to Webster, "I have lost a dear friend and an honoured master, and there is no one to take his place." One of the least expected tributes disclosed a little-known interest of Ganong's. Rendell Roades, of the Ohio Division of Conservation and Natural Resources, wrote to Smith: "The obituary of Dr. Ganong in a recent issue of *Science* came with some surprise. I knew Dr. Ganong only through his early works on the natural history of New Brunswick. He was one of the few men living in our time who has made a contribution to our knowledge of freshwater crayfish. His position among men of this interest was worthy of great respect. We join the many others who lament his death." In 1886, Ganong had written short articles for the *Bulletin* in 1886 on crayfish—freshwater lobsters—in the streams of Charlotte and Victoria Counties.

Scientific journals carried obituaries and notices and, aware of Ganong's failing health, the editors of the *Journal of Plant Physiology* dedicated the January 1941 issue to him. The previous year the American Society of Plant Physiologists had awarded him the Charles Reid Barnes Life Membership. Historians and geographers, however, were silent. Ganong had never joined the Association of American Geographers, and in eastern Canada there were few professional geographers and no professional association or journal until 1950. Nor were there geography departments in any of the Maritime universities. As Michael Caron pointed out, a prominent physical geographer at McGill, unaware of Ganong's annual field excursions and his seventy-five articles for the *Bulletin* on physiography and topography, commented in 1972 on the lack of physiographic studies in the Maritimes. Historians were silent for other reasons. Ganong's wasn't the kind of history then in vogue, and in truth history was not his best subject. As a regional historian and a particularist with antiquarian tendencies, he had no interest in forging a Canadian identity or contributing to a philosophy of history. Nor was he interested in writing about socio-political, cultural, and economic developments, subjects then beginning to engage Maritime historians. Obituaries for both the *Canadian Historical Review* and the *Transactions of the Royal Society* were written by Clarence Webster.

The most complete exposition of the compartmentalization that, at least in part, led to the neglect of Ganong's oeuvre came from Lawrence Martin, Chief of the Map Division at the Library of Congress in Washington, who did not know that a close friend of his wife was married to the eminent cartologist:

> *Few geographers interested in cartography knew that Ganong was eminent as a botanist and that his principal work was in that field. Conversely, I suppose many botanists do not know of his work in cartography and other allied geographical subjects. We at the Library of Congress are filled with admiration at the competence and diligence with which Ganong was able to pursue his studies in connection with such subjects as the boundaries of New Brunswick, the historic sites in that province, the evolution of place names on maps of New Brunswick*

and the Maritime Provinces of Canada, and the sources of successive maps from an original type which Ganong worked out so brilliantly. His series of monographs on crucial maps in the early cartography and place nomenclature of the Atlantic coast of Canada constitutes one of the most important contributions in this field ever published in America.

Clarence Webster's public tribute to Ganong was at the first Founders Day ceremony held at UNB since the 1860s. Originally conceived as a day for honouring distinguished graduates and associates of the university, the practice had languished until revived to honour Ganong.

The Ganong Library and Reading Room at the New Brunswick Museum.
NEW BRUNSWICK MUSEUM: NBM-450-3

The day chosen for the 1942 ceremony, February 17, was two days before Ganong's birthday. For the benefit of students and faculty who might not have been aware of the range of Ganong's achievements, Webster spelled these out forcibly. Ganong was the province's most distinguished scholar and an acknowledged authority on its natural history, its settlement history, Aboriginal place nomenclature, physiography, and cartography. In all of these, where few had preceded him, he conducted basic, pioneer research. Webster went on to note that for him, Ganong's death was a deep personal loss. Ganong was a man of the highest character and one of the most modest men he had ever known. Honours, rewards, and publicity were of little interest, and the honours he did receive were not sought. Royalties from his textbooks aside, his writing brought him no financial gain. All expenditures for books, maps, travel, and documents came out of his own pocket. To end his address Webster turned to poetry. First Kipling's stirring "When Earth's Last Picture is Painted," a choice that pleased Anna, for Ganong admired Kipling:

> *They shall work for an age at a sitting and never be tired at all!*
> *And only the Master shall praise us, and only the Master shall blame;*
> *And no one shall work for money and no one shall work for fame.*
>
> *But each for the joy of working, and each, in his separate star*
> *Shall draw the Thing as he sees It for the God of Things as They are.*

And, finally, George Meredith's elegiac quatrain from the novel *Vittoria:*

> *Our life is but a little holding, lent*
> *To do a mighty labour: we are one*
> *With heaven and the stars when it is spent*
> *To serve God's aim: else die we with the sun.*

ACKNOWLEDGEMENTS

First, my thanks to Jennifer Longon, Christine Little, and Amber McAlpine-Mills, keepers of the voluminous William Francis Ganong Collection at the New Brunswick Museum Archives in Saint John, for many months of cheerful, unstinting service. Jennifer Longon, who worked on the catalogue of the collection, is a deep well of information on all matters relating to Ganong. The archivists at Smith College, too, who provided material on the history of the college gardens and the botany department, during my visit to Northampton, could hardly have been more attentive and accommodating.

My largest single debt of thanks, however, is to Stephen Clayden, head of botany and mycology at the provincial museum. In a fine, balanced article in a special supplement to the Museum's magazine—which in some ways was the catalyst for this book—he deplored the neglect of Ganong and appealed for a fuller, lengthier study of the man and his work. This is not the fuller study Stephen envisaged, but it will at least make up for some of the neglect. Stephen also read and commented on the chapters in this book on botany and ecology. Responsibility for any errors or omissions in those chapters, however, or in the remainder of the book, is mine alone.

SELECTED PUBLISHED
WRITINGS BY W. F. GANONG:
A TIMELINE

A complete list of Ganong's publications may be found in J. Alan Rayburn's *A Compilation of Books, Papers, Notes and Reviews Written and Edited by W. F. Ganong between 1864 and 1941* (Secretariat of the Canadian Permanent Committee on Geographical Names, Fredericton, April 1968). The theses by Michael Caron and Mary Sanger also have extensive bibliographies.

BOTANY AND ECOLOGY

1891
"On Raised Peat Bogs in New Brunswick." *Botanical Gazette,* May: 123–6.

1894
"Beitrage zur Kentniss der Morphologie und Biologie der Cacteen," Ph.D. dissertation, University of Munich.
"An Outline of Phytobiology." NHSNB *Bulletin* 12: 1–15.

1895
"Present Problems in the Anatomy, Morphology, and Biology of the Cactaceae." *Botanical Gazette* 20, 1895: 129–38, 213–21.
"The Botanic Garden of Smith College." *Smith College Monthly,* December.

"Laboratory Teaching of Large Classes in Botany." *Science* 1, 9, March.

1897
"The Lyman Plant House." *Smith College Monthly* 4, 6, March.
"The Botanic Garden of Smith College." *Garden and Forest* 10,
December.
"Upon Raised Peat Bogs in the Province of New Brunswick."
(Contributions to the Plant Geography of New Brunswick, No. 1),
Royal Society of Canada (rsc) *Transactions*, Sect. IV: 131–9.

1898
"Upon Raised Peat Bogs in the Province of New Brunswick." rsc
Transactions 2nd series, Volume 3, Section 3: 131–63.
"Contributions to a Knowledge of the Morphology and Ecology of the
Cactaceae, the Comparative Morphology of the Embryo and the
Seedlings." *Annals of Botany* 12, 48: 423–74.

1899
"Some Appliances for the Elementary Study of Plant Physiology."
Botanical Gazette 27, 4: 266–7.
The Teaching Botanist. New York: MacMillan.

1901
A Laboratory Course in Plant Physiology, Especially as a Basis for Ecology.
New York: Henry Holt.
"The Cardinal Principles of Morphology." *Botanical Gazette.* 31, 1901:
426-434.

1902
"The New Laboratory and Green House for Plant Physiology at Smith
College." *Science* 15, April: 933–7.

1903
"The Vegetation of the Bay of Fundy Salt and Diked Marshes: An Ecological
Study." *Botanical Gazette* 36: 161–86, 280–302, 349–67, 429–55.

1904

"New Normal Appliances for Use in Plant Physiology." *Botanical Gazette* April 1904, Feb. 1905, March 1906, April 1907, Oct. 1909.

"New Precision Appliances for Use in Plant Physiology." *Botanical Gazette* 37, April: 303–7. Also 39, February 1905: 145–52.

"The Cardinal Principles of Ecology." *Science* 19: 493–8.

1906

"The Nascent Forest of the Miscou Beach Plain." *Botanical Gazette* 42, August: 81–106.

1907

Botanical Apparatus for Use in Plant Physiology. Bausch & Lomb Optical Co.

1909

"The Identity of Animals and Plants Mentioned by the Early Voyagers to Eastern Canada and Newfoundland." RSC *Transactions*, 3rd series, vol. 3, section 2: 197–242.

1910

"Some Reflections upon Botanical Education in America." *Science* 31, March: 321–34.

"The Place of Botanic Gardens in Collegiate Instruction." *Science* 31, 644–48.

1913

The Living Plant, a Description and Interpretation of its Functions and Structure. New York: Henry Holt.

1916

A Textbook of Botany for Colleges. London: Macmillan.

1917

"The Botanical Equipment of Smith College; A Study in Educational Adaptation." *Smith Alumnae Quarterly* 8, 3: 183–91.

ZOOLOGY

1885

"On the Invertebrate Animals of Passamaquoddy Bay." NHSNB *Bulletin* 4: 87–97.

"Summer Camp, with Notes on the Marine Invertebrates of L'Etang Harbour and the Neighbouring Waters." NHNSB *Bulletin* 5: 34–36.

1887

"The Marine Mollusca of New Brunswick." NHSNB *Bulletin* 6: 2–45.

"The Crayfish in New Brunswick." NHSNB *Bulletin* 6: 74–75.

1888

"The Echinodermata of New Brunswick." NHSNB *Bulletin* 7: 12–68.

1889

"The Economic Mollusca of Acadia." NHSNB *Bulletin* 8: 3–116.

1890

"Southern Invertebrates on the Shores of Acadia." RSC *Transactions* 8, 4: 167–85.

1909

"The Identity of Animals and Plants Mentioned by the Early Voyagers to Eastern Canada and Newfoundland." RSC *Transactions*, 3rd series, vol. 3, section 2: 197–242.

NEW BRUNSWICK HISTORY

1891

"The St. Croix of the Northeastern Boundary." *Magazine of American History* 26, October: 261–5.

1895

"A Plan for the General History of the Province of New Brunswick." RSC *Transactions*, second series, vol. 1: 91–102.

1896

"A Monograph of the Place-nomenclature of the Province of New Brunswick." RSC *Transactions*, vol. 2, section 2: 175–289. And vol. 12, 1906: 4–57.1898:
"The Ashburton Treaty." *New Brunswick Magazine* 6: 297–305.

1899

"A Monograph of Historic Sites in the Province of New Brunswick." RSC *Transactions*, second series, vol. 5, section 2: 213–357. And vol. 12, 1906: 77–150.

1901

"A Monograph of the Evolution of the Boundaries of the Province of New Brunswick." RSC *Transactions,* 2nd series, vol. 7, section 2: 139–449.

1902

"Dochet (St. Croix) Island – a Monograph." RSC *Transactions*, second series, vol. 8, section 2: 127–231. Revised and enlarged by S. B. Ganong as *Ste. Croix (Dochet) Island,* New Brunswick Museum, 1945.
"On the Use and Value of Historical Museums." *Acadiensis* 2, April: 131–5.

1904

"The Great New Brunswick Survey, a Daydream." *Acadiensis* 4, January: 76–79.

"Champlain's Narrative of the Exploration and First Settlement of Acadia." *Acadiensis* 4, July-October.

"A Monograph on the Origins of Settlements in the Province of New Brunswick." RSC *Transactions*, second series, vol. 10: 3-185.

1905

"New Brunswick Animals and Animal Romancers." NHSNB *Bulletin* 23: 299–304.

1906

"The Meaning of the Day." Maine Historical Society's *Collections*, third series, vol. 2: 57–76.

"History of Miscou." *Acadiensis* 6, April: 81–94. Revised and enlarged by S. B. Ganong, New Brunswick Museum, 1946.

"History of Tracadie." *Acadiensis* 6, July: 185–200.

"A Monograph of the Cartography of the Province of New Brunswick." RSC *Transactions*, second series, vol. 3, section 2: 313–427; vol 12: 57–76.

1907

"History of Caraquet." *Acadiensis* 7, April: 91–114. Revised and enlarged by S. B. Ganong, New Brunswick Museum, 1948.

"History of Pokemouche." *Acadiensis* 7, January: 9–26. Revised and enlarged by S. B. Ganong, New Brunswick Museum, 1946.

"History of Tabusintac." *Acadiensis* 7, April: 314–32.

1908

"History of Neguac and Burnt Church." *Acadiensis* 8, October: 267–87.

"History of Shippegan." *Acadiensis* 8: 138–61.

1911

"An Organization of the Scientific Investigation of Indian Place-nomenclature of the Maritime Provinces of Canada." RSC *Transactions*, third series, section 2, vol. 5: 179–93; vol. 6, 1912: 179–99; vol. 7, 1913: 82–106; vol. 8, 1914: 260–92; vol. 9, 1915: 376–448.

COASTAL SUBSIDENCE

1905

"An Absolute Measure of the Rate of Recession of the New Brunswick Coast Line." NHSNB *Bulletin* 5, 23: 306–8.

1906

"On the Physical Geography of Miscou." NHSNB *Bulletin* 5, 24: 456.

1908

"The Physical Geography of the North Shore Islands." NHSNB *Bulletin* 6, 26: 22–29.

"On the Physiographic Characteristics of Portage and Fox Islands, Miramichi." NHSNB *Bulletin* 6, 24: 20.

1910

"An Absolute Measure of the Rate of Recession of the New Brunswick Coast Line." NHSNB *Bulletin* 6, 28: 216–8.

1912

"On the Stability of the New Brunswick Coast." *Saint John Globe*, June 10.

HISTORICAL CARTOGRAPHY

1887

"Jacques Cartier's First Voyage." RSC *Transactions*, vol. 1, section 2: 121–36.

1889

"The Cartography of the Gulf of St. Lawrence from Cartier to Champlain." RSC *Transactions*, vol. 3, section 2: 17–58.

1904

"Champlain's Narrative of the Exploration and First Settlement of Acadia." *Acadiensis* 4: 179–216.

1964

Crucial Maps in the Early Cartography and Place Nomenclature of the Atlantic Coast of Canada. Toronto: University of Toronto Press, 1964.

TRANSLATING AND EDITING

1905

Lescarbot, Marc. *History of New France.* Vol. 2. Translated and edited by W. L. Grant. Introduction by H. P. Biggar with notes by W. F. Ganong. Toronto: Champlain Society.

Smethurst, Gamaliel. "Narrative of an Extraordinary Escape out of the Hands of Indians in the Gulph of St. Lawrence." NBHS. Collections 2, 6: 358–90.

1907

W. F. Ganong, "Richard Denys, Sieur de Fronsac and His Settlements in Northern New Brunswick." NBHS. Collections 3, 7: 7–54.

1908

Denys, Nicolas. *The Description and Natural History of the Coasts of North America.* Translated and edited by W. F. Ganong. Toronto: Champlain Society.

1910

Le Clercq, Father Chrétien. *New Relation of Gaspesia with the Customs and Religion of the Gaspesian Indians.* Translated and edited by W. F. Ganong. Toronto: Champlain Society.

1922

The Works of Samuel de Champlain. Vol. 1. Translated and edited by H. H. Langton and W. F. Ganong. Toronto: Champlain Society.

1937

Campbell, Patrick. *Travels in the Interior Inhabited Parts of North America.* Ed. H. H. Langton and W. F. Ganong. Toronto: Champlain Society.

PHYSIOGRAPHY AND NATURAL HISTORY

Ganong's 150 papers for the *Bulletin* of NHSNB, written between 1884 and 1917, and the annual field trips that gave rise to them, are listed in Nicholas Guitard's book, *The Lost Wilderness.* A typescript briefly describing each of Ganong's field trips may be found in the New Brunswick Museum: S222 F 56-1.

ASSESSMENTS OF BOTANY AND ECOLOGY

For assessments of Ganong's contributions to botany and ecology readers may consult the following:

Cittadino, Eugene. *Nature as the Laboratory: Darwinian Plant Ecology in the German Empire, 1880–1900.* Cambridge: Cambridge University Press, 1990.

———: *Ecology and the Professionalization of Botany in America, 1890–1905*, Volume 4 in Studies in the History of Biology. Baltimore: Johns Hopkins University Press, 1980.

Kohler, Robert E. *Landscapes and Labscapes, the Lab-field Border in Biology.* Chicago: University of Chicago Press, 2002.

McIntosh, Robert P. *The Background of Ecology, Concept and Theory.* Cambridge: Cambridge University Press, 1986.

Young, C. Mary. *Nature's Bounty: Four Centuries of Plant Exploration in New Brunswick.* Fredericton: University of New Brunswick, 2015.

BIBLIOGRAPHY

Few scholars as prolific as W. F. Ganong have received so little attention. The first book about him, Nicholas Guitard's *The Lost Wilderness*,
appeared just over a year ago, in 2015. Until then, the only written items
were two theses, one book chapter, and a handful of articles. These are:

Bell, John and Gary T. Whiteford. "Exploring New Brunswick with W.
    F. Ganong," *Canadian Geographic Journal*, 99, 1979: 38–43.

Caron, Michael B. "A Reconnaissance of Particularism in the New
    Brunswick Studies of William Francis Ganong." Master's thesis,
    University of Kansas, 1978.

Clayden, Stephen. "William Francis Ganong." *New Brunswick Museum
    News*, Special Supplement, Fall 1991.

Guitard, Nicholas. *The Lost Wilderness, Rediscovering W. F. Ganong's New
    Brunswick.* Fredericton: Goose Lane Editions, 2015.

Lane, M. Travis. "An Interview with Alfred Goldsworthy Bailey." *Studies
    in Canadian Literature* 11, 2, 1986, 226-245.

Marquis, Greg. "The Story of a Map: W. F. Ganong and Tribal
    Boundaries in New Brunswick." Papers of the 39th Algonquian
    Conference, University of Western Ontario, 2008.

Mitcham, Allison. *Three Remarkable Maritimers*. Hantsport, Nova Scotia: Lancelot Press, 1985.

Sanger, Mary E. J. E. "William Francis Ganong, Regional Historian." Master's thesis, University of Maine, 1980.

Webster, J. C. *William Francis Ganong Memorial*. Saint John: New Brunswick Museum, 1942.

Wynn, Graeme S. "W. F. Ganong, A. H. Clark, and the Historical Geography of Maritime Canada." *Acadiensis* 10, 2, 1981: 6–28.

PRIMARY SOURCES

W. F. Ganong. Correspondence, 1889–1941: New Brunswick Museum.

————. Field journals, 1880–1929, scrapbooks, notes, questionnaires, photographs. New Brunswick Museum.

————. "Historical Geography of New Brunswick." New Brunswick Museum.

Pierce, A. H. Field journals, 1896–1912. New Brunswick Museum.

Smith College Archives. Grounds collection, botany department, and faculty files.

SOURCES ON SMITH COLLEGE

Immerman, Gaby. "Landscapes for Learning." *Botanic Garden News*, Smith College, Fall 2011: 11–12.

Neilson, William Allan. "Smith College: The First Seventy Years" (unpublished typescript, ca. 1946). Smith College Archives.

Seelye, L. C. *The Early History of Smith College, 1871–1910*. Boston: Houghton Mifflin, 1923.

OTHER WORKS

Goldthwait, J. W. "Supposed Evidences of the Subsidence of the Coast of New Brunswick within Modern Time." Canada Geological Survey, *Museum Bulletin* No. 2, Geological Series No. 15, 1914: 1–23.

Johnson, D. W. "Botanical Phenomena and the Problem of Recent Coastal Subsidence." *Botanical Gazette* LVI Dec. 1913: 449–69.

MacDougall, Pauleena. *Fannie Hardy Eckstorm and her Quest for Local Knowledge 1865–1946.* Orono, ME: University of Maine Press, 2013.

INDEX

Numbers set in italics refer to images.

MORE FROM
RONALD REES

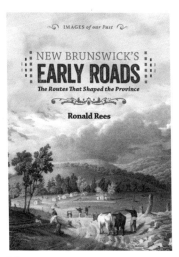

New Brunswick's Early Roads
978-1-55109-934-7

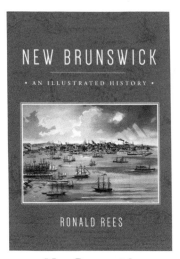

New Brunswick:
An Illustrated History
978-1-77108-152-8

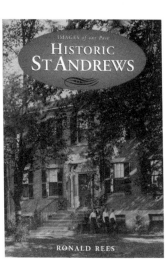

Historic St. Andrews
978-155109-357-4

Land of the Loyalists
978-1-55109-274-4